THE GOLD TREASURE OF INDIA

THE GOLD TREASURE OF INDIA

AN ENQUIRY INTO ITS AMOUNT THE CAUSES OF ITS ACCUMULATION AND THE PROPER MEANS OF USING IT AS MONEY

CLARMONT DANIELL

GYAN

Published by

Gyan Publishing House
5, Ansari Road
Daryaganj, New Delhi-110002
Phone: 011-47034999, 9811692060
E-mail: books@gyanbooks.com

Distribution Network
gyanbooks.com
India, USA, Canada, UK, Australia

ISBN: 978-93-7225-535-5 (PB)

First Published, 1884

2nd Impression 2026

Printed at: Gyan Press, Delhi.

THE GOLD TREASURE OF INDIA
Author: CLARMONT DANIELL

THE GOLD TREASURE OF INDIA

THE GOLD TREASURE

OF

INDIA

AN ENQUIRY INTO ITS AMOUNT
THE CAUSES OF ITS ACCUMULATION
AND THE PROPER MEANS OF USING IT AS MONEY

BY

CLARMONT DANIELL, B.C.S.

FELLOW OF THE CALCUTTA UNIVERSITY

LONDON
KEGAN PAUL, TRENCH & CO., 1 PATERNOSTER SQUARE
1884

CONTENTS.

THE GOLD TREASURE OF INDIA.

INTRODUCTORY.

THE tendency of the precious metals to accumulate in Asia, has long attracted public attention, and certain classes of people are described by economists to have suffered a loss, not easily perceptible, but nevertheless actual, and in the aggregate of considerable dimensions, from an enhancement in the value of gold as against commodities, during the last few years. While the drain of gold from Europe and America shows no sign of diminishing, the Government of India is constrained to spend about thirty millions more of its silver or rupee revenues, in purchasing sovereigns for the settlement of its liabilities in England, than would be necessary if gold were lower or silver higher in value when exchanging with one another than is the case at present.

So far as the amount of this sum depends on a remediable over-valuation of gold, it might be reduced by additions to the stock of that metal available for use as money.

So far as it depends on the depreciation of silver in the gold valuation, any measure tending to bring into use the discarded silver money of the European world would tend to raise its value.

An endeavour is therefore made in the following pages to sketch the history of the precious metals in connection with the trade between India and foreign countries from the earliest ages, to describe the causes always in operation which directed the course of gold and silver to India, to estimate the stock of gold which has been under process of accumulation in India during more than twenty-five centuries, and to urge (not for the first time) on the consideration of those interested in this subject the importance of liberating the vast gold treasure hoarded in India (which the following observations will show to exceed considerably £200,000,000 in value), and, by making it available for use as money, to reduce the value of gold as a purchasing agent to its natural proportions.

For the scheme discussed in these pages there is also claimed this effect, that it will provide a stimulus to the use of silver by widening the foreign market for the productions of India, and by increasing the capacity of her people to purchase manufactured goods from the West; and that it will generally encourage the use of silver as coin by making it interchangeable with gold on terms which preclude either metal obtaining any advantage over the other, the interchange of the gold and silver current coin being strictly regulated by the intrinsic value at which for the time being the one stands to the other.

PART I.

MINES OF THE ANCIENT WORLD.

THE sources from which the nations of antiquity in Western Asia and Europe supplied themselves with the precious metals, were the washings of a few rivers principally in Spain and Asia Minor, and excavations from below the earth by slave labour in the same countries, and in Greece, Nubia, and Northern Arabia.

The legend of Cadmus opening a gold mine in Thrace in (if chronology can in such a case be relied upon) the sixteenth century B.C., the myth of the expedition of Jason to Colchis on the eastern shore of the Euxine and through the Ægean sea to the islands of the Mediterranean, and other similar adventures of Phœnician gold-finders, are among the earliest traces we find of the pursuit of this form of wealth.

Diodorus, writing in the first century B.C., speaks of an inscription in a palace at Karnak, in Egypt, recording the annual revenue of the king who placed it there to amount in gold and silver to a value equivalent to £6,000,000. The gold was probably obtained from Nubia, or sources still further south in Western Africa; and the rocks of Midian are known to have yielded gold, and southern Arabia gold and probably silver in small quantities. From all of these countries the kings of Egypt doubtless derived revenues of the precious metals. The explorations of the Phœnicians in Spain led to the opening of mines by their Carthaginian colonists, which, from the fifth to the second century B.C., provided those nations in Europe who were sufficiently civilized to use money, as well as the Phœnicians, the Egyptians, the people of Babylonia, and the Indians, with silver for that purpose. The silver mines of Laurion, in Attica, appear to have been closed about 500 years B.C., while those in the island of Samos were worked as late as the second century of the same era.

That silver and gold were used as money at the dawn of history is evident from the purchase by the patriarch Abraham of the cave of Machpelah with "shekels of silver current with the merchant." A statement in the code of the Egyptian Menes of a ratio of value existing between gold and silver, and regulations in the institutes of Menu, the Hindu lawgiver, for the payment of interest on money lent under risk, and for the insurance of goods against loss in transit, imply a recognized use of the precious metals as money—by weight, at least, if not in the form of coin—at a very early period in the history of the three most ancient nations in the world.

The Phrygians are said on an authority somewhat doubtful to have coined gold and silver between the fourteenth and twelfth centuries B.C.; and from an age not much later the Lydians are ascertained to have done the same, their gold being obtained from the Pactolus and other rivers of Asia Minor, and their silver from the mines of Thrace and Attica.

Mr. Del Mar, the historian of the precious metals, to whose work I am indebted for some of the information on which the conclusions in this treatise rest, is of opinion that gold and silver money first came into Europe from India, through the intervention of the Phœnicians. The commercial relations which that people held with the Aryan inhabitants of India, and the fact that a ratio of value in the exchange of the two metals was recognized on the shores of the Mediterranean so long ago as the fifteenth century before our era, are in favour of this theory.

The use of token money by the Romans previous to the middle of the third century, by the Greeks up to the commencement of the fourth century B.C., and by the Carthaginians at an earlier period, is an incident in the history of this subject which is worth noticing, in proof of the antiquity of this method of economizing the use of the precious metals, and because it accounts for what is from other sources known to have been the case, that silver and gold were transported from the places of their production as merchandise, and in that form were exchanged by the Tyrians in their land and sea trade for the commodities of India and the further East.

Distribution of the Precious Metals.

In the old world when commerce and the arts of peace were in their infancy, one of the most cogent motives to international wars is found to have been the acquisition of mines, and the treasure accumulated in the temples of the gods and the palaces of the wealthy. To both Punic wars the Romans were principally impelled by the desire to possess themselves of the precious metals which the Carthaginians drew from the mines of Spain and the islands of Sicily, Sardinia, and Corsica. After about sixty years of warfare, the destruction of the Carthaginian power was completed by Scipio, about the year 200 B.C., and the treasures of the Carthaginian cities in northern Africa, and the mines of Spain, and those three islands, were incorporated in the dominions of the Roman Republic.

Alexander the Great obtained a treasure by the invasion of Persia and India calculated at £50,000,000 by weight, and having a purchasing power vastly greater than that of modern money.

The nucleus of this treasure was probably that which Darius, about one hundred years before, had plundered from the Phœnicians, whose cities were filled with the wealth they had amassed in exchanging the silver of Carthage for the silks and spices of India, and from the spoil of Asia Minor and Egypt. This monarch levied a tribute on his conquests to the west of the Euphrates equal to £3,000,000; and although his successors were unable to enforce its punctual payment, the fact that the Tyrians, who were amerced in the larger part of this fine, should have undertaken to pay it, argues the highly profitable and extensive character of their trade with the East, from which the wealth for which they were famous was principally derived.

In every condition of the political world outside Asia, whether peace reigned and commerce flourished or war convulsed society and brought nations to ruin, India continued to appropriate the metallic treasures of the West; and the movement of that stream of gold, silver, lead, tin, and iron, to that country, which commenced nearly three thousand years ago, has never been interrupted, but has constantly and progressively increased in volume and intensity. Our own generation is, in consequence, witnessing such an accumulation of gold in India as no nation of the ancient or modern world has ever, at one time, possessed.

Because (to borrow an aphorism from Edmund Burke) the superfluities of a rich nation furnish a better object of trade than the necessities of a poor one, the frugal and industrious Indian exchanged the silks, cottons, spices, and jewels of his own country, for which he had little need, against the overflowing treasure of silver in Tyre, Carthage, and Rome, and of gold in Egypt, Arabia, and Persia, in preference to seeking smaller profits with greater toil on the sale of mere necessaries to his poorer neighbours in Asia.

The climate of India, and the character of its inhabitants, allowed of the production within her own borders of every thing which her people required for their own sustenance. She desired nothing which foreigners could give her but the precious metals. Gold and silver India was in need of for the fabrication of coin and for purposes of luxury. These redundant and therefore comparatively useless treasures were necessarily willingly surrendered for merchandise of that description, which India and the East alone could supply. The pursuit of the arts, and habits of luxury and ostentation, had for some centuries before the Christian era made such progress among the people of Western Asia, Northern Africa, and those parts of Europe which had easy access to the Mediterranean Sea, that fashion and caprice no less than certain peculiarities in their religious rites combined to invest these commodities with a factitious value. These circumstances fully account for the drain of the precious metals from all parts of the ancient world, and from America in modern times, into India.

PHŒNICIAN OR TYRIAN, JEWISH, AND BABYLONIAN TRADE ROUTES

The history of commerce, both in the ancient and modern worlds, presents us with the noteworthy fact that, in the case of every nation which has at any time engaged in trade with the East, the highest point of development which its domestic civilization and political influence attained has corresponded with the period when that commerce was most flourishing.

It will serve the purposes of this essay to give a brief account of the routes by which each people in turn succeeded in giving this commerce a direction to their own coasts, since the necessary result and fruit of these efforts was, by supplying the people of India with ample stores of the precious metals for use as money, to give them the means of creating a highly civilized system of social order and an elaborate and extensive commerce, at a time when the people of Greece and Italy had not appeared as organized powers on the world's political stage.

Solomon perceived that which has since become more evident to mankind, that the trade with the East speedily enriches the nation which for the time succeeds in obtaining its control. Egypt, no doubt, was to Solomon the visible evidence of this fact, and he addressed himself to appropriate as large a share of it as he could for the Jewish people, by creating facilities for traders with the East on both the land and sea routes.

Solomon's schemes to this end were evidently designed in concert with the Phœnicians, for the joint advantage of that people and the Jews. He built Tadmor, which the Greeks afterwards called

Palmyra, at a distance of one hundred and twenty miles from the Euphrates, on the edge of the Syrian desert, probably Baalbec (Heliopolis) also, and Hamath (Epiphania), as store cities; that is to say, to serve as resting-places for caravans travelling from Persia, Babylonia, and the head of the Persian Gulf, and as emporia at which the camels' burdens were sorted and arranged for distribution. From Tadmor part of the merchandise would be carried to Palestine, from Baalbec and Hamath to Tyre, Aradus, and other Phœnician ports on the Mediterranean, to the cities in the valley of the Orontes, and to the port at the mouth of that river, subsequently named Seleucia, or by way of Edessa and the valley of the Euphrates into Asia Minor. The wealth of the inhabitants of Lydia, and of other parts of the west coast of Asia Minor, which five hundred years after the era of Solomon excited the cupidity of Xerxes, was, we may reasonably conjecture, partly derived from the Eastern trade, especially as they held, in the gold-bearing sands of their rivers, the surest means of attracting its course into their cities.

Solomon's foresight in protecting these caravan routes bore fruit in the creation of the great trading centres of Mesopotamia. Babylon, Ctesiphon, Seleucia, Ossis, and Borsippa, at different times between his age and that of the Roman Emperor Severus, rose to importance, flourished and decayed on the profits of their commerce with Asia.

The spoil obtained by Alexander the Great in his victories over the Persians about 340 years B.C., and that taken at the sack of Ctesiphon by the Musalman, General Khaled, in the year 637 A.D., consisting principally of the productions of India or of such commodities as were exported to the West by way of India from more distant countries, testify to the source from which that part of Asia enriched itself. The length of time during which this commerce flourished gives us the means of estimating the amount of the treasure which India must have acquired in the exchange.

The power of Tadmor, or Palmyra as it was latterly called, rested on foundations laid by Solomon, and after the decline of the Babylonian cities, succeeded to their commercial and political importance.

Appian, writing during the first century A.D., describes the Palmyrenes as buying commodities from the Arabians and Parthians, and selling them again in Rome.

Palmyra appears to have attained its highest point of prosperity at a period corresponding with the decline of the Roman Empire. In A.D. 260, Odenathus, the prince of that city, and husband of Zenobia, was sufficiently powerful to contend with

Sapor the Persian for the possession of his prisoner, the Emperor Valerian. Thirteen years later, the Emperor Aurelian, conquering Palmyra and capturing its Queen Zenobia, found in the city an immense treasure of precious stones, gold, silk, and cotton goods, commodities which could only have been obtained by trade with Persia, India, Ceylon, and countries still further eastward.

As Solomon used his power to promote the success of the land trade of the Phœnicians, the King of Tyre assisted him with shipwrights and sailors to equip and man the navy of ships which he "made at Eziongeber, which is beside Elath, on the shore of the Red Sea in the land of Edom;" that is to say, in the eastern arm of that sea now called the Gulf of Akaba. This fleet made periodical voyages, from which it is inferred that it sailed at seasons when the monsoon winds blowing off the coast of Africa would serve for the outward voyage to the western coasts of Asia. The region called Ophir—probably a term of general application, taking its name from a district in Arabia, and indicating, as the word "Indies" in modern times, different emporia for eastern productions—is described as the object of its voyage; but it seems unlikely that India was included in that term. The merchandise of the East having been conveyed to Elath, and thence by caravan to Petra, was distributed—some to Egypt; some to a port on the Mediterranean in the angle between that country and Palestine, which in Strabo's time was called Rhino Colura, for the purpose of exports to Europe; and the rest was taken partly to the Phœnician cities north of Palestine, and partly into Palestine itself. Petra like Palmyra grew rich as the emporium of this trade; historians both sacred and profane, describe its magnificence; and its monuments, which are of a late period of Greek art, attest the length of time during which the commercial system originated by Solomon preserved its vitality. It was not until the reign of Trajan that the importance of this city declined under the competition of Alexandria.

The islands of Tylos or Tyros, and Aradus in the Persian Gulf, which are now called Bahrein, and are probably identical with the Daden of Scripture, were believed by the Greeks to have been the cradle of the Phœnician people. Tradition is hardly likely to be wrong on this point, confirmed as it is by the use of these islands as emporia for the Tyrian carrying trade. That the Tyrians should have called two of their principal ports on the Mediterranean coast of Syria by the names of these two islands, gives much probability to the theory, as colonists ever love to call the new cities they found in strange lands by the familiar names of their distant homes. There, and at the neighbouring port of Gerrha, on the main land which the geographers describe as one of the richest cities of its day, the Tyrians collected the merchandise brought into the gulf by coasting vessels from India. Arabian caravans travelled by a road passing to the north of the great desert, through the inhabitable tract now occupied by the State of Nejd, and over the Djebel Shomer to Petra; but the Phœnicians organized the transport of commodities by sea and river from Gerrha and Aradus, to various points on the Euphrates, whence they were taken by way of Palmyra into Syria, as has been above described.

That Solomon's navy, with the assistance of these people or in concert with them, since the Phœnicians are described as making voyages from Gerrha round Arabia into the Red Sea, sailed from the same port touching at other places in the Persian Gulf, at Aden (the Uddin of Isaiah), and the coasts of Western Arabia, and so to Elath, can be a matter of no reasonable doubt. It was only by voyages to these parts that his ships could have collected the tribute from the "princes of Arabia," or the revenues collected by "the governors of the country," and that derived "from the traffic of the merchantmen," which are spoken of in Holy Writ as the principal means of that monarch's magnificence; and we need go no further than the ports on the seas which washed the coasts of Arabia for an explanation of the voyages of the Jewish navy to Ophir.

The Phœnician race, considering the age of the world during which they flourished, and the rudimentary state of general knowledge on the subject of astronomy, navigation, and the art of shipbuilding which prevailed at that time, have been surpassed by no modern nation in commercial enterprise. They pushed their trade in new and unexplored countries and ransacked the known world for mercantile commodities. The Persian Gulf to this day retains traces of their cities. In Africa, Carthage Utica and less important provinces were colonized by them; they had visited Italy and established themselves in Sicily, Crete, the Balearic and other Mediterranean islands some centuries before the age of Romulus; beyond the pillars of Hercules Gades (Cadiz) was one of their seats of trade; and the district of Tartessus, on the river of that name, which the Arabs afterwards called Guadalquivir,* was a Phœnician colony. A name of Aryan origin indicating the possession of tin mines, which was afterwards adopted by the Greeks, was probably bestowed by mariners of the same race on the inhabitants of

* Wadi-'l-kebir is in Arabic, "the great river."

the Scilly Isles and the Cape of Cornwall. They were the first of the nations of antiquity to link together in one commercial system all countries sufficiently civilized for trade which lay between Ceylon, and perhaps China, in the east, and Britain in the west. The territory of the different cities which comprised the Phœnician power extended for only eighty or ninety miles on the northern sea coast of Syria; of these Aradus, Tripolis, Berytus, Sidon, and Tyre were the first in rank; but so numerous along the coast were the seats of Tyrian industry and commerce that the inferior maritime towns presented the appearance of an almost continuous series of harbours, habitations, wharves, warehouses, and temples. Phœnicia held the same place among the commercial powers of antiquity that Venice held in the Middle Ages and England holds now. Each state in its turn has organized trade between the east and the west, and carried most of it in its own navies. By directing the main streams of commerce on to its own shores, each has become for the time the principal agent for exchanging the goods of one half of the world with those of the other half, and has thereby given its people the means of accumulating vast wealth from the profits of trade with every country lying between its own borders and either verge of civilization.

The palmy days of Tyrian prosperity are believed to have been attained under their King Hiram, the contemporary of the Jewish kings David and Solomon, whose era was probably 1000 B.C.; it waned under the attacks of the Persian kings in the sixth century B.C. Alexander's conquest of the city 332 B.C., and the success of his scheme for diverting the Indian trade through Egypt and the port of Alexander into Europe, dissipated the commercial ascendancy of Tyre. In the age of the Ptolemies it had ceased to be of much importance as trading centre in the Levant.

Egyptian Trade Routes.

The Egyptian monuments ascribed to the age of Sesostris, which record his naval battles, are interpreted as illustrating the wars waged by that monarch against the maritime tribes of Arabia, with a view to appropriate for the benefit of his own people the sea trade which they carried on between their own coasts and those of Asia and Africa. This theory derives support from the construction of a canal by Sesostris between the Nile and Arsinoë, at the head of the Gulf of Suez. This work, however, probably from the difficulty of keeping it clear of silt, seems never to have been much used by large vessels. The Ptolemies reopened it, but at the same time provided three other routes for the passage of merchandise imported into Egypt from India and the Persian Gulf, which would not have been resorted to if the canal was capable of carrying ships of burden.

The most favourite route from the Red Sea started from Berenice, the harbour formed by the promontory of Ras Benass, and touched the Nile at a distance of one hundred and seventy miles at Coptus, near Thebes (Karnak). To the same point there was a shorter but, passing through rocky country, probably a more difficult route of eighty or ninety miles from the port now called Kossier. A second led from Myos Hormos (Aboo Shaar), a roadstead at the entrance to the Gulf of Suez, which probably struck the river at the modern town of Sioot. From these ports goods were carried by land to the Nile. A third route led through the desert from Arsinoë to a town a little north of the ancient Memphis, built on or near the site where modern Cairo now stands. This would, therefore, be the same route as that used for the conveyance of the Indian mails to Europe before the railway between Suez and Alexandria was opened.

The people of Egypt flourished on the Indian

trade equally under the dynasty of the Ptolemies and under the rule of the Roman emperors. The destruction in turn of the Phœnician, Jewish, and Persian power in Western Asia gave to the seamen of Egypt and Arabia a monopoly of this commerce for about the space of nine hundred years, between the death of Alexander the Great and the conquest and occupation of Egypt by the Arabian followers of the prophet under Amrou, the general of the Caliph Omar, in A.D. 640. The discovery of Hippalus in the first century A.D. (if the fact were not known before), that a voyage could be made with tolerable safety, and with a calculable certainty as regards the length of time required for its completion, between the entrance of the Red Sea and the western coast of India, by utilizing the periodical winds which blow across the Indian ocean, allowed ocean sailing vessels to dispense with the necessity of coasting. Either this circumstance or some improvements in the construction and navigation of ships during the occupation of Egypt by the Romans gave an impulse to trade and the mercantile marine of the Egyptians, which in those days was regarded with wonder. The statement which Heeren quotes from Strabo (who was a contemporary of the Emperor Tiberius), describing himself as having seen as many as one hundred and twenty ships of burden engaged in the

Indian trade lying in the roads of Myos Hormos at the same time; and the incident recorded in the history of the reign of the Emperor Aurelian, about two hundred and forty years later, that after the reduction of Palmyra he was obliged to turn his arms against Egypt to suppress an insurrection which was supported by Firmus, a merchant of that country, with a fortune he had made in the trade with India, are circumstances which argue that at this period of the world's history, as in every other age, the golden stream of commerce flowing from India enriched every country whose shores it touched; and that in exchange for their productions, the people of that country continued to appropriate a large part of the metallic treasures of the civilised world, which at that time had become the possession of the people of Arabia, and of Egypt, and of the nations inhabiting the shores of the Mediterranean sea.

ITALIAN AND OTHER EUROPEAN TRADE ROUTES.

For nearly two hundred years the Oriental trade of Egypt languished under the dead hand of Musalman rule, until the Venetians, about the year 800, allying themselves with the Turks, revived the use of this route.

This people laid the foundations of the great carrying trade, upon which the Italian Republics flourished for seven hundred years between the ninth and sixteenth centuries. The conquest of Constantinople in 1204–5, by the Latin crusaders, to which the Venetian fleet, under the command of the famous Dandolo, mainly contributed; the acquisition by the Republic of territory on the mainland of modern Turkey, of Crete, and other important islands and places of advantage for trade in the Levant, made her commercial supremacy paramount wherever the sails of European merchantmen were seen.

The commercial history of Venice is much mixed up with that of Genoa, and with that of Catalonia in Spain, with both of which she was frequently in rivalry; and with that of Florence, whose port was Pisa. Venice provided Germany through the intervention of the merchants of Augsburg, and countries lying nearer Italy, with Oriental productions, principally obtained by means of her navies sailing from the coasts of India to Egypt, through which country a system of land and river transport was organized to Alexandria, whence they were re-shipped across the Mediterranean.

Genoa, in the time of the Greek emperors, obtained an influence at Constantinople which gave her the command of the Bosphorus, and ensured her the monopoly of one branch of the commerce of the East, which came by an overland route of great antiquity from the direction of the Caspian sea.

This course of trade appears to have followed two lines of country, one mentioned by Herodotus which conveyed gold from the Imaus range and the western frontier of China (Thina), and the peltries collected by the tribes between those mountains and the northern shore of the Caspian, through the country of the Scythians and Sarmatians to the north shore of the Black Sea, where the Greeks had already in his time placed trading stations; the other to have united at a pass situated under the thirty-fifth parallel N.L., called the Caspian Gates, two caravan routes, one starting from Western China and the countries situated between the Himalayas and the southern shore of that sea, and another travelling from India in a direction nearly west from Kandahar. A third route appears to have passed from India through Media, or through northern Assyria into Asia Minor, and to have supplied the wares of Asia to the colonies which the city of Miletus had, between the seventh and fifth centuries B.C., planted on the shores of the Euxine, from Sinope to Dioscurias.

Heeren's researches leave no doubt that commercial relations brought into communication with one another in prehistoric ages the nations and tribes of northern

India, North-western (or, as it is commonly called, Central) Asia, Persia, Mesopotamia, and the territories now forming Southern Russia. In the Middle Ages the Genoese transported merchandise conveyed to the Black Sea by these long established channels from a port called Caffa, on the sea of Azof, in their ships to northern Europe, the Netherlands, and the Baltic.

The skill and enterprise of the Medici raised the Republic of Florence to a point of singular prosperity, both commercial and political.

The basis of the gigantic fortune of that House was a share in the trade of the East, coming probably by some channel where its influence was supreme, such as an overland route through Syria, or Armenia and Asia Minor, which would have lost its exceptional advantages when ships began to make voyages round the Cape of Good Hope.

Ormuz, in the Persian Gulf, Aden, and apparently Kossier in the Red Sea, were the principal stations for the Venetian sea-borne trade with India, and these they secured by a formidable navy of armed commercial vessels. From Alexandria they re-shipped the merchandise for distribution along the coasts of the Mediterranean, or for transport to Venice and Genoa, whence it was exported into the interior of Europe. The Venetian occupation of

Cyprus, for nearly one hundred years during the fifteenth and sixteenth centuries, gave them facilities for organizing another route for the conveyance of the Indian trade by the Euphrates, and by land from that river through Syria to the ports on the northern coast of Palestine. The total destruction in the Indian sea in the year 1508, by the Portuguese admiral, of a combined Turkish and Venetian fleet, which those two powers had equipped for the purpose of extinguishing the rivalry of the Portuguese in the Indian trade, and the appropriation by the same people of the Venetian stations at Ormuz and other places in the Gulf, deprived the Republic of her carrying trade in Eastern waters; while the greater security and cheapness of the voyage round the Cape of Good Hope involved a simultaneous disuse of every overland route, either through Egypt, Syria, or the country between the Caspian and Black Seas, and reduced the commerce of the Italian and Levantine cities to unimportant dimensions.

The appointment of Albuquerque, in 1506, as Governor on the part of the King of Portugal in the Indies, speedily confirmed the value of Vasco de Gama's recent discovery of the sea passage round Africa to India, by substituting that nation for the Venetians as the carriers of the Oriental trade.

In the year 1595, the merchants of Amsterdam

fitted out their first India fleet of armed trading ships, to contend with the Portuguese for a share of this commerce. The destruction of the city of Antwerp, ten years before, by the Duke of Parma, had driven a considerable number of artisans, merchants, and others interested in trade, from the Low Countries to take refuge on the banks of the Thames.

It is from that time that England, as well as Holland and Portugal, began to freight ships for the voyage round the Cape with a certain amount of merchandise, but with disproportionately large stores of silver and gold, derived from the recently discovered sources of supply in Central America, and to bring to Europe in exchange cotton, pepper, silk, and other rarities and articles of luxury from the coasts of India.

This route has only during the last forty years been partially given up in favour of the more rapid means of transport which ocean steam ships, a railway, and a ship canal through Egypt, now offer to a commerce carried in the vessels of every nation of the world which owns a mercantile marine.

Indian Trade Routes in Asia.

Besides the inhabitants of the countries situated to the west of India, those of Central Asia, Thibet, China, the Straits of Malacca, and the countries on the eastern coasts of the Bay of Bengal, traded with her people: and as in ancient times the inhabitants of those regions possessed gold and silver, it is not only probable, but historically certain that they put their treasure to its most profitable use, that of effecting commercial exchanges, and thus contributed an additional supply to the stores of the precious metals accumulating in that country.

Ctesias, a Greek physician, who lived at the Persian Court about 400 B.C., while (like many other writers of an uncritical age of historical research) he records much that is fabulous, may nevertheless be considered an authority on such matters as modern history has shown to be possible. He speaks of that which is the oldest recorded trade route connecting the countries lying between the Caspian and India on the west, with Tartary and China on the east, as being frequented by caravans of a thousand or two thousand men travelling through a desert, which must be that now called by the name of Cobi, and returning in three or four years, their beasts being laden with gold. Ptolemy, the geographer, writing in the second century of our era, speaking of probably the same route as that described by Ctesias, says that merchants travelling from Parthia and Bactria followed a road which lay under the same parallel of latitude as Byzantium (42°) to the country of the Seres (China), from the capital of which people that metropolis was seven months' journey. This route is traceable from the mention by Ptolemy of a certain stone tower which Heeren believes to be identical with a building mentioned by travellers as existing in 1780—a fortified caravanserai called Chahel Situn, or the forty columns, placed to guard a pass apparently in the Alai Mountains, about three days' march south-east of Marjilan, on the road from Khokand to Kashgar, and therefore near the town of Ush or Oosh. This route is probably still used, as it was more than two thousand five hundred years ago by those visiting the countries beyond the sandy desert which stretches eastward from Aksu and Khoten. Heeren identifies both of these towns with places bearing Greek names in the itinerary of this route.

The gold, silk, furs, and other commodities brought on to the borders of India by these caravans appear to have been collected at Taxila, the modern Attock, in the Punjab, and thence distributed throughout the interior of the country. One course of trade was directed to a point on the Jumna, in the neighbourhood of the modern Delhi, a district which, as the vast extent of ruins in that neighbourhood attest, has from remote ages surrounded a succession of populous cities, built nearly on the same site.

Following the Doab of the Ganges and Jumna, it probably descended the former river to Palibothra (which is now known to be represented by the city of Patna), the capital of the people whom the Greeks called Prasioi. This city, the most magnificent of its age, flourished for about one thousand years, from 500 B.C. to some date between 400 and 600 A.D.

At the height of their power, about the time that Megasthenes visited their king Chandragupta (B.C. 300), this people had extended their dominion over countries which are now included in modern Bengal, between Sirhind and the mouths of the Ganges, and between the Himalayas and Central India. To refer to this circumstance is hardly a digression, as the existence of so powerful a nation during so long a period of time argues the maintenance of a strong government and a durable and highly organized polity, which are ever found to promote the growth and secure the extension of internal and external commerce with the necessary result of attracting the precious metals from foreign countries. As will afterwards be seen, part of the merchandise so conveyed passed on to the mouths of the Ganges, and thence to the Çoromandel coast and Ceylon.

Another line of trade started from Taxila, and went down the Indus to Patala on the delta of that river, whence it was conveyed by the coast to the sea ports in the Persian Gulf.

It appears likely that a land route for merchandise passed from Taxila through North-western India to Ozene or the modern Oojein in Malwa, and to a city called Pluthana, and to another called Tugara in Central India, whose sites are uncertain. The sea port for that part of India was Barygaya (Broach) at the mouth of Nerbudda, whence an active trade was kept up with both coasts of the Persian Gulf in correspondence with the commerce in the precious metals from Europe, Arabia, and Egypt, which the Phœnicians conducted by means of their trading stations in the Arabian waters; and with the inhabitants of the Assyrian and Mesopotamian cities, who forwarded their wares by caravan and river to the mouths of the Euphrates.

The materials from which Ptolemy, the geographer, compiled in the second century A.D. his itineraries afford proof that in the age of Alexander, and certainly during many preceding centuries, a great commerce was carried on between India and Ceylon on the one hand, and Burmah, Siam, Malaya, and the coasts and islands lying to the south and east of the Straits of Malacca as far as China on the other. Nearchos, exploring under the orders of Alexander the coasts of the Persian Gulf, found a settlement where Muscat now stands, in communication with Limyrica (the Malabar coast of India) and Ceylon. Commodities are described in the "Periplus" as being conveyed down the Ganges and thence sent to Limyrica; and the author of that work (writing *circa* A.D. 64) mentions a town called by the same name as that river, situated near its mouth, which served as a trade emporium. Merchandise from the east coast of the Bay of Bengal would, at most seasons of the year, be carried into or past the Ganges, according to the part of India, eastern or southern, which might be its destination, and two streams of trade would thus unite on their way to the Coromandel coast, the chief port of which was situated at the mouth of the Cauvery.

From Ceylon commodities collected from the mainland of India and from countries to the east of the bay were distributed along the western coast by vessels issuing from many different ports between the southern cape of India and the delta of the Indus. Heeren quotes Agatharcides, who wrote about one hundred and fifty years before our era, as noticing the importance of Patala near the mouths of the Indus in the trade between India and Arabia. Calliene (Callian near Bombay) is mentioned in the "Periplus" as a port which had recently decayed after a long career of prosperity. Barygaya, or Broach, has already been noticed. Musiris, in Limyrica, where stands the modern Mangalore, was resorted to by Greek traders at the commencement of our era for the purchase of silk.

Pliny describes the ships frequenting the ports of Ceylon as square-built vessels, whose timbers were not fastened with iron, but sewn together with cocoanut or some similar fibre; a description which in one respect applies to the junks used by the Chinese, and in another to the masulah boats which ply on many parts of the Coromandel coast. The "Periplus"* (quoted by Irving) describes silk as being brought to that port from Thina (which is believed to indicate North-western China) by caravans to some point on the Ganges, and necessarily by that river to the sea, and thence to Ceylon. This and other commodities from the same region may either have travelled round the sea coasts of Asia, *viâ* the

* The "Periplus of the Erythrean Sea" is believed to have been written in the reign of Nero, *circa* A.D. 64, by Arrian, an Egyptian Greek, who is not to be confounded with Arrian of Nicomedia, the historian of Alexander's expedition to India, who was Governor of Cappadocia (*temp.* Hadrian A.D. 136).

Straits of Malacca and the Bay of Bengal, to that island, or have been conveyed by land and river transport from Northern India to the mouths of the Ganges, and thence have been taken by the Coromandel coast, which was well provided with small but convenient ports, to its destination in the southern sea.

Cosmas Indicopleustes, an Egyptian traveller, who in the sixth century B.C. compiled from the narrative of one Sopater, who had visited India, an account of the commerce of Ceylon, notices the activity of the trade along the coast of Limyrica, and describes it as issuing from Ceylon, which was the principal emporium for that part of Asia, and being transported in vessels belonging to numerous ports on the coast, which he names—among which Nel Kynda (identified by Heeren as the modern Neliceram) and Arrhota (Surat) still exist—to the Persian Gulf.

In this way the merchandise of China, Southern Asia, and India, fell into the courses of commerce through which the seamen of Arabia and Egypt and the caravan traders of Assyria distributed it throughout the Roman Empire.

That commerce between distant places within India and adjacent countries was organized long previously to those times which Greek accounts of the country refer to, is to be gathered from ancient books in the dead languages of India, from incidental notices of the Tyrian trade in the Jewish scriptures, and other historical sources, as well as from the character of the commodities which were imported into Western Asia and Europe from the East.

Character of the Indian Trade.

The social semi-religious code of the Hindus, called the Institutes of Menu, which, if the age of its compilation be much more recent than that attributed to it by the people themselves, must be held to contain regulations whose authority had become confirmed by the acquiescence of many generations; speaks of a class of "men well acquainted with sea voyages and journeys by land, and of ship-builders, and of sailors, as many as navigate rivers." To a particular caste of Hindus was assigned the business of conducting trade, and upon them was enjoined the necessity of making themselves acquainted "with the productions and requirements of other countries, with various dialects and languages, and with whatever else has direct or indirect reference to purchase and sale." *

* Irving's "Commerce of India."

The use of coined money and the practice of insuring goods in transit against risk were, as we have seen, common in India many centuries before our era. The economy of coined money effected by a system of banking and the use of bills of exchange is also known to be of great antiquity in that country. These circumstances add fresh corroboration to the general evidence regarding the length of the ages during which her inhabitants have drawn from all quarters of the world a supply of the precious metals for use as money.

Besides gold, the importation of which into India will be noticed separately, there were collected from foreign countries in Asia, or produced within her own boarders for export to Europe, such merchandise as could be easily transported on beasts of burden and in the ships of small tonnage in use in ancient times, but which was at the same time sufficiently rare to command a high price abroad.

High Asia and the mountain range, called by the Greeks Paropamisus, which is comprised in the territories of Affghanistan, Badakshan, and Kashmir, supplied wool from the fleeces of a breed of sheep which were as famous in the time of Alexander as they are now. This was carried to Borsippa near the Euphrates, and there woven into material; or further still to Tyre, to be steeped in the dye of the

Murex. The ancient celebrity of the Milesian fleeces is considered to be largely owing to a mixture of this Indian wool with that locally produced.

From the Imaus range came the onyx calchedony, and similar stones used for signet rings; lapis lazuli and jasper, regarded as precious stones by the ancients; and a resinous gum, deposited by an insect on the bark of certain trees as shell-lac is formed by the cochineal beetle at the present day in the central Indian forests.

The mountains to the north and west of India supplied, as in our day, furs, asafœtida, and the aromatic secretion of the musk deer.

The towns in the same region furnished embroidered woollen fabrics and coloured carpets, the former of which were as highly prized in Babylon and Rome as they are now in modern Europe under the name of Kashmir shawls; while the latter were used more for decorative than useful purposes, as hangings for the walls of palaces and temples, like the arras of the Middle Ages.

The most valuable merchandise, however, from Eastern Asia was silk, which, under the Persian Empire, was exchanged by weight with gold. It is at the same time little less than certain that silk of Indian manufacture, as well as that obtained from China, was sent beyond India, as the manufacture of the fabric has long been indigenous in those parts of the country where the climate permits the breeding of silkworms. From Northern India were imported cotton fabrics of many varieties, graduating between the finest muslin and calico to the coarsest cloth. Sindon was the name given by the Greeks to cotton fabrics generally, some qualities of which are said to have been esteemed by the Persians as hardly less valuable than silk. Oils, brassware, a liquid preparation of the sugar cane, drugs, and dyes were procured from various parts of the country. Gerrha, the Tyrian emporium in the Persian Gulf, was famous for the export of salt, which was doubtless procured from India, where the manufacture and trade in the condiment has always flourished.

Of the Tyrian trade with India, surviving written accounts are but meagre, and only incidentally met with in a few Greek and Hebrew writers. The prophecy of Ezekiel, which is partly taken up with predictions of the destruction of the Phœnician polity, contains an allusion to the Tyrian merchants trading "in all sorts of things, in blue clothes, and broidered work, and in chests of rich apparel bound with cords, and made of cedar." These words are interpreted to refer to the cotton stuffs dyed in indigo, and the embroidered silks and woollens of China and India. The latter would, no doubt, be distinguished by being packed in chests of hard wood (which is pronounced to be the only certain interpretation of the word rendered by "cedar"), secured with cords of fibre, a method still in use for merchandise from China and the Straits, instead of being made up in bales and fastened with ropes of twisted horsehair for conveyance on camels and other beasts of burden.

From Ceylon especially, as well as from other parts of Southern and Western India, were imported into Europe, Egypt, and Asia west of India, various kinds of valuable spices, both for consumption as food and to supply the demand created by the use of aromatics in mortuary and sacrificial rites. Of the former, cinnamon and pepper were held in most account; while sandal-wood from India and China, and camphor from the latter country, were used for the latter purposes. Cordage and canes for use in the rigging of ships were productions of Ceylon and of the islands of the Archipelago eastward of the Malacca Straits.

From the export of these commodities, and from that of the ivory of elephants which roamed wild in the hills, of ebony from the forests, and pearls from the shores of the island, the merchants of Ceylon and those of the neighbouring mainland of India supplied themselves with gold and silver, in addition to that which the hilly parts of the island undoubtedly produced.

The trade which passed through the hands of the Singhalese during many centuries could only have been organized by the Government of the island having the control of ample supplies of the precious metals, which its inhabitants are known to have possessed in great abundance.

Gold in Ceylon.

Although the age which produced the Ramayana may be much more recent than that to which the Hindus ascribe its composition, its antiquity is unquestionable; and the description in that epic of wealth in gold both manufactured and in use as money, possessed by the people of the countries mentioned in it, among which Ceylon was the most conspicuous, proves that the precious metals must have been generally diffused among the nations of India from a very early period of their history; and as the supplies from local mines were limited, they can only have obtained their gold and silver from foreign countries.

Megasthenes, who visited India about the year 300 B.C. and travelled as far east as the modern Patna, describes Ceylon as producing gold; and Cosmas was informed that the traders from Ceylon obtained the metal in exchange for merchandise at the port of Adule on the Red Sea, and from Yemen in Southern Arabia.

Pliny speaks of the people of Ceylon finding gold among their hills; and the ambassadors sent by the King of Ceylon to the Emperor Claudius (*circa* 41–54 A.D.) excited curiosity and wonder by their description of the luxury and magnificence of their monarch, to which a lavish use of gold, not only in personal decoration, but in the enrichment of buildings, largely contributed.

That both Southern India and Ceylon obtained gold and silver from China may be certainly inferred from the fact of that country having always possessed and generally exported those metals, especially gold, of which India has received from that quarter large supplies; while the Greek names of Chrysa and the golden Chersonese, applied to the Burmah and Siamese coast and to the Malayan peninsula, attest that those regions were as famous for the production of gold at the commencement of our era as they are now for its possession and use.

GOLD IN NORTHERN ASIA.

Only scanty notices indicating the particular sources of gold supply in Northern Asia are met with in ancient authors.

The gold of the Imaus and of a region (the Thina of the "Periplus") on the north-western border of China, has already been noticed, as being the basis of a caravan trade between Upper Asia and India. Herodotus speaks of a tribe on the banks of the Jaxartes among whom utensils of gold were as common as Pizarro found them to be among the Mexicans on the discovery of America. Strabo and Arrian describe what can be nothing else, when stripped of the guise of fable, than the practice of excavating gold from beneath the earth by a people who inhabited the borders of the desert of Cobi and wore clothing of hides, a peculiarity in which they are imitated by a remote Himalayan tribe at this day. As these gold-diggers were periodically robbed by visitors using horses and carts to carry off their spoil, we may conclude that they were armed traders from India who relieved them of the fruits of their labour. The satrapy of India, which included as much of Affghanistan, Kashmir, and the Punjab, as the Persian monarchs could keep in subjection, was esteemed a dependency of great importance, by reason, among others, of the gold dust in which its tribute of three hundred and sixty talents was paid, a fact which can only be accounted for by the importation of gold into that region from Central Asia, whence Ctesias and Herodotus record that it was usually brought in the age of Darius Hystaspes.

Travellers who have recently visited that part of Central Asia lying nearest to India find that the drain of two hundred and forty centuries has not exhausted its beds of gold. The narrative of the mission sent to the Amir of Kashgar by the Indian Government in 1873–74, speaks of some of the envoy's staff witnessing the annual arrival of tribute at the capital, either presented in person or despatched by the governors of distant districts in the province; the tribute and offerings consisting of the productions of each locality. Among them the Governor of Khoten "led in a caravan of four hundred and fifty camels laden with carpets, silks, cottons, felts, tents, metal dishes, and other local manufactures; two arabas (carts) each carrying 1500 jings (equal to about 1800 pounds) of gold and silver," and some other contributions of less consequence.

GOLD IN SOUTHERN INDIA.

While India was thus levying contributions of the precious metal on every nation in Europe or Asia with whom she traded, some considerable quantities of gold were obtained by superficial mining in the hills of the Deccan. The researches of Mr. E. B. Eastwick into this subject have recently made known to us such information of this source of supply as the most ancient records contain. The inscription on the great temple of Tanjore is quoted to prove that in the eleventh century A.D. gold was more common in Southern India than silver. Mahmoud of Ghazin (1017–24) took away, as the plunder of his frequent expeditions into India, a considerable treasure from Mathura on the Jumna, and from Somnath in Guzerat—in that age the principal seats of the Hindu religion—and from Kanouj on the Upper Ganges, the capital of a powerful state. The rise of the Mahomedan states of Central Asia is probably attributable to these acquisitions.

The Hindu princes, on the other hand, of the Deccan, as masters of the country which had produced and, at that time, retained large quantities of gold, fell victims to the cupidity of the Mahomedan conquerors of Northern India, who, during and subsequent to the fourteenth century, transferred to their own capital of Delhi a considerable part of this treasure. That empire reached its climax of power in the sixteenth and seventeenth centuries. In the year 1738, Nadir Shah, a Persian adventurer, sacked the city, and is said to have appropriated £6,000,000 sterling in specie, and to have levied a contribution of £8,000,000 more on its inhabitants.

These figures, however, are of no statistical value, because the modern equivalent of the standard of value used by the annalists of these monarchs is very uncertain, and because their object in compiling their narratives was not so much to record history as to glorify their masters by exaggerating the magnificence of their conquests. The same author bases a theory that the six hundred and sixty-six talents of gold recorded as coming to Solomon in one year (2 Chron. ix. 3) was an annual tribute, and levied on the produce of the mines of Southern India, on the assumption that the Ophir of Scripture and India are the same place; and he argues that that monarch drew from India some £160,000,000, or on an average £4,000,000 a year during his reign, which never returned to the country at all. The question of the locality to which the name Ophir was applied is fully discussed in Smith's "Dictionary of the Bible," and the conclusion to be drawn from all that is known on the subject is, that that region comprised the gold yielding districts of Arabia, and perhaps Ethiopia, where gold was also found. The almug trees which the navy of Hiram brought from Ophir have not been identified with any timber known to us, and they cannot, therefore, be assumed to have been grown in India. The navy of Hiram, which in concert with that of Solomon, brought gold, silver, ivory, apes, and peacocks, once in three years into the territory of the Jewish monarch, is not recorded as making the voyage to Ophir, and it is not safe to assume that the apes and peacocks were procured either from Ophir or India. If the terms of 1 Kings x. 22 are to be understood in their exact sense, it would seem that Tarshish gave its name to this triennial voyage ; and if that region was (as it probably was) the Tartessus of the Phœnicians, it was situated in South-western Spain : and the precious metals and the curiosities mentioned in this passage were more likely to have been brought from the coast of Africa and from Madeira than from anywhere else. The argument for India derived from the use of the word "peacocks" is but of little weight, as commentators agree that the word in the original implies a bird remarkable for a long tail, a peculiarity which peacocks share with parrots, pheasants, and other birds. This revenue

E

of six hundred and sixty-six talents cannot, therefore, be assumed to have been furnished from Indian gold. Nor is it certain that it was an annual tribute, and therefore no safe reckoning can be made of what it amounted to during the forty years that Solomon reigned. There can also be no doubt that whatever treasure was accumulated in Palestine by the offerings of the kings* of Arabia, the tribute collected by the governors of provinces, and taxes levied on merchants, must have gone into circulation as money among the people. The trade of Solomon's subjects—in all ages a people with the strongest commercial instincts—the mention of which in Scripture proves it to have been of remarkable extent and value, and the enormous expenditure involved in the administration of a territory extending from Anti-Libanus to the Red Sea, and from Egypt to the Euphrates, could only have been maintained by a general diffusion of the precious metals among the people of those countries, and by their constant employment as money in internal trade and foreign commerce. So far, then, as the treasures of Solomon may have been indirectly derived from India, there can be no doubt that the share which that country contributed to them found its way back to her merchants and producers in the ordinary

* 2 Chron. ix. 13.

course of business, and it cannot be held as probable that India lost a single ounce of gold by reason of her commerce with the Tyrians and Jews.

CAUSES ATTRACTING THE PRECIOUS METALS TO INDIA.

The simple habits of the people of India, a fertile soil and genial climate, make them independent of foreign nations for the necessaries and for most of the luxuries of life. The list of commodities from abroad, which could have at any time found a sale in India, is a very short one. Tin, lead, and glass, and probably amber, were imported by the Tyrians in one age, and the Venetians in another, and the latter may have supplied steel for arms, and medical drugs, while frankincense for use in the temples was procured from Arabia. There is good reason to believe that slaves were for many centuries an article of traffic in this trade. The large part that domestic slavery played in the social life of the ancient world, and the practice among successful generals during the latter days of the Roman Republic and the Empire of selling the people of conquered tribes into slavery by the thousand, makes this highly probable. The custom of dealing in human beings with the people of Asia is believed to have prevailed up to a late period in the era of Christianity. Besides these commodities, there remained nothing that the people of the country could want, except the precious metals. However large the quantity of foreign merchandise may have been which could be profitably imported into India, there must always have remained a heavy balance due for goods exported from India, which could only have been settled by the surrender of those stores of the precious metals, of which the indebted nations had an abundant supply.

Drain of Gold to India.

The drain of gold and silver from Europe to the East has been a matter of complaint against the Indian trade at all times. Carthage, in the fourth century B.C., used to dispose of the silver and gold which she procured from Spain by sending it to India through the intervention of the Tyrians. At that time both that State and Rome used little or no silver for money. The importation of Carthaginian silver into Italy and the importance of the Indian trade were no doubt the exciting causes of the Punic wars, two hundred years later. Pliny relates that in his time (first century A.D.), while the export of the precious metals was frequently and in vain prohibited from the Roman Empire, a sum of money equal to £3,000,000 was annually exported into India. So well was this peculiarity of the trade known in modern times, that in the charter granted by Queen Elizabeth to the first English East India Company, in the year 1600, it was stipulated that the associated merchants were "to import, within six months after the return of every voyage, as much gold and silver as shall be equal to the value of the silver exported by them." This regulation was, from the nature of the case, but feebly enforced, and soon repealed. As early as the year 1674–75, the accounts of the Company showed that out of their exportations to India, to the value of £550,000, £400,000 was entirely bullion. Del Mar is of opinion that in the three hundred years between the middle of the sixteenth century and our own time, £160,000,000 of gold and £440,000,000 of silver were exported from Europe and America to the East, which has never been re-exported; but as he obtains this figure by making a deduction for treasure taken by the Portuguese and Dutch from Japan, between 1545 and 1646, in the amount of £70,000,000, which was certainly indigenous to that country, and for some other withdrawals of treasure from the East which was not likely to have been altogether obtained from the West in the first instance, and as this author's estimate does not include the net importations of treasure into India during the last seven years, an addition of £200,000,000 may safely be made to his estimate of £600,000,000, as evidence of the drain of gold and silver to the East in comparatively recent times. The value of the vast treasure imported into India from foreign countries, during the last two generations, is too well known to need particular mention here. That this current of the precious metals has set towards the East, without intermission, for twenty-five centuries, is a conclusion which is historically certain, and which our knowledge of the ordinary operation of the laws of trade make it impossible to deny. To gold all the world is a home; it is an unwelcome stranger nowhere. It flows into all countries where it can be profitably used, however distant they may be from the source of its supply, as surely as water runs down hill. It has in consequence, from a remote antiquity, been employed in India as an instrument for exchanging the productions of countries far distant from one another. Its abundance has been evident through all historical times, in its lavish use for purposes of State and personal adornment, in the magnificence of the public buildings and the palaces of the rich in all parts of the country. It is still retained as hoarded treasure by wealthy men of all classes, and in the case of most bankers and traders doing a large business, it serves as a basis to their credit as merchants.

CAUSES REGULATING THE EXCHANGE VALUE OF MONEY. THE STABILITY OF VALUE OF GOLD.

As, however, the succeeding pages of this treatise will be chiefly occupied with the discussion of a proposal to circulate gold and silver coins in the Indian currency at a varying ratio of exchange, it will not be irrelevant to consider what the conditions are on which the value of money, when used to exchange commodities, depends.

Owing to the imperishable nature of gold, and to the care which people ordinarily take of it, the stock of the metal existing above the earth's surface is liable to but little diminution in amount by attrition, loss in manufacture, or accident. Its homogeneous character allows of its division into parts, the values of which are ordinarily in the same proportion to one another as their weights. The rarity of the metal permits a large value to be carried in a small bulk; and as its durability allows the same coin to be used many times over, a smaller quantity of the metal serves for the exchange of a vastly larger quantity of goods than would be required if a more perishable material than gold were used as money. The accumulations made by previous generations are thus maintained, but little impaired in amount, and the total mass of metal available for money increases yearly faster than it diminishes. While, on the one hand, the producers and owners of gold are under a constant inducement to add to the world's stock of the metal in quantities limited only by the ability of mankind to find it, on the other hand the continuity of the demand for gold for use as money gives to it a steadiness of value in the exchange with other commodities, which no other production of nature, or of human labour and skill applied to such productions, in the same degree possesses. Most commodities which come within the range of commerce are produced for sale at some point of time in the immediate future. They are either perishable in their nature, or they may become wholly or partially valueless by a change of fashion, or from supersession by some other article of more use in the same field of employment. In many cases, the owners of such goods are under a necessity to sell them in order to realize the profits of their business. But none of these conditions affect gold. The demand for it in the form of coined money is ordinarily in advance of the supply; any quantity hitherto produced has not proved to be more than adequate to the work which it has to do. As it requires a greater force to disturb the equipoise of a large than of a small mass in suspension, so, owing to the magnitude of the accumulations already existing, the yearly increment of fresh money to the stock in use has little or no influence on the equilibrium of value which gold holds to commodities. The owners of gold therefore feel no apprehensions that the article they have to sell will greatly decline in value, diminish in amount, or be with difficulty put on the market when they wish to dispose of it.

Another reason why gold alters less in value against commodities than commodities alter against one another is, that, except in the case of the acquisition of gold in river-beds and similar situations on the surface of the earth—a source of supply which is soon exhausted—increased quantities of gold excavated from mines are obtained at a constantly increasing expenditure in wages of labour and machinery. In the manufacture of most articles, a continuity of demand induces improvements in labour-saving machinery, which reduce the prime cost, or increase the out-turn, in direct correspondence with the increase in the capital laid out on the machinery. This is the case, however, in a less degree when improved and more costly machinery is applied to the excavation of gold. The use of the machine may facilitate excavation of the ore, but the miner cannot be sure that gold will be found where the machine is set up; nor is the quantity of the metal excavated increased, or the cost of its production lessened, in any certain ratio to the amount of capital invested in the enterprize.

Taking one mass of metal with another, each 100 lbs. weight of gold taken out of the mines costs more in every way to bring it to the surface than the last; and to secure to the miner the return of his capital with a fair amount of profit, each fresh supply of gold is put on the market in exchange for an increasing quantity of other commodities.

These circumstances all contribute to secure to gold money its characteristic steadiness of value. No production or commodity is so rare and obtainable under conditions which vary so little from time to time as to secure to it absolute fixture of value; but in the case of the precious metals, the closest approximation to this condition is reached by gold.

As silver possesses all the characteristics of gold

in a lower degree than that metal, it is proportionately less convenient as a measure of value, and therefore as a medium of exchange. While we say of any merchandise, which may cost £5 at one season and £6 at another, that it has risen in value 20 per cent., the same could not be affirmed with certainty if the price had varied from 500 to 600 pieces of silver in a market where silver might be in use as money in free circulation with gold. In the latter case it is the silver which would have fallen in value against merchandise if the price of the latter in gold remained unaltered. It is of importance to bear this in mind, in considering the circumstances of the currency of India, the greater part of whose exports, although they are purchased with silver in that country, are immediately after sold for gold in Europe or America, and whose commercial balances, as those who reside in that country know to their cost, are settled in silver at a valuation based on the market price of that metal in gold.

COST OF PRODUCTION, ITS INFLUENCE ON THE VALUE OF MONEY.

Gold, like other commodities, can only be converted from its crude form to man's use by human labour. (It will save repetition if in this place it is stated that in the term labour are included the food and wages of workmen, the cost of machinery, of buildings, of carriage, and of anything else indispensably necessary to placing gold as bullion or as money in the market.) But the distribution of the metal beneath the earth's surface, even in places where it is comparatively abundant, is very capricious. Mining adventures are in a large proportion of cases failures, but the search for gold occasionally rewards the labour of a few hours with such a quantity of the metal as will exchange in the market for commodities many times exceeding in value those which the same efforts could have procured in any other field of industry, while the difficulties which the situations in which it is found present to its excavation generally result in the labour bestowed upon mining being much less productive than it would have been if applied in other ways; nevertheless, the hope of a sudden and vast return to a moderate amount of toil continues to attract capital to an enterprise which is, on the average, comparatively unremunerative, and will continue to do so as long as the gambling spirit forms a constituent of human character. If any given number of sovereigns could be traced to their parent nuggets, it would be often found that they had cost more in labour than they could at the first exchange have purchased. The failures in mining largely preponderate over the successes. As the bulk of the metal is put on the market at less than the ordinary profits on the employment of capital in commerce, the exertions of the owners of the larger quantity are always directed to keeping up its price—that is, to exchanging it away for as large a share of the necessaries or luxuries of life as they can obtain; while the more fortunate owners of the smaller and more easily acquired portion are equally unwilling to part with their prize except on as good terms as other gold-owners in the same market can command.

Gold, like iron or coal, is but a commodity. When one man sells goods for gold, the purchaser sells gold for goods, and as the gold is the equivalent of the labour primarily bestowed on its production, the sale is in effect a sale of those goods for the labour which produced the gold; and because traders exchanging their wares for one another do so at such an estimate of their relative values in each case as will compensate each purchaser and seller for what he has expended on his share of them respectively, it follows that under a system of free competition in production and sale all commodities, gold included, exchange for one another ultimately, and, on the average, on the basis of the cost of their production. Again, all men in the pursuit of commerce, equally among a primitive people exchanging their goods by the method of barter, or among a civilized people using the precious metals as money, seek to get something of a higher value than that which they give in the exchange. Thus, the seller of goods for money when he spends it endeavours, if he is a trader, to make a profit on its investment in the purchase of fresh goods. In doing so he exchanges one kind of commodity or produce for another, and the latter, in some way or another, brings him more advantage than he could get if he had retained the former. Thus every increase in the quantity of commodities produced, by being itself exchanged for some other commodity still more in request, tends to excite in its turn a still larger and increased production of the objects of human desire. The gold which is the medium of effecting these exchanges is of no use to the persons in whose hands it may temporarily rest until it is converted into some other commodity, which can again be sold at a profit. Gold being the machinery which keeps the current of exchange in motion, has the appearance of stimulating production, but it is, in fact, the demand for increased commodities which is the real stimulus. Gold being itself a commodity produced by labour, exchanges for other commodities of the same value as those which were expended in its own production, and it necessarily exchanges for them on the same basis on which they in the long run exchange for one another, namely, the cost of its production.

If in free competition gold or any other article is exchanging for other goods which cost less labour in their production than the quantity of it offered for them cost, other producers seeking to obtain a share of the excess of profit over the ordinary returns to capital employed in trade will supply the market with larger quantities of the article in question, and thus by lowering its value tend to redress the balance of advantage in favour of those who hold the merchandise of inferior value. While this operation is in process, the oscillations in the amount of profit which those on either side of the exchange may earn may be frequent and variable, but a force has been set in motion which tends to correct the alternate elevations and depressions that the values of the commodities in exchange exhibit, and which ultimately reduces them to the level determined by their common cost of production.

The influence of the law of the cost of production is exerted more directly in the case of that portion of the precious metals used in the arts than that which is used as coined money, and, as will be afterwards seen, its operation is modified when the law of supply and demand begins to act upon them in the latter character; yet, even as money, gold and silver are amenable to its regulation, as may be seen in respect of the silver money of our own day. While it is needless in this place to inquire into the causes which have induced a fall in the value of silver money in some parts of the world, it is sufficient for the purposes of the present argument to remark that a much larger quantity of silver must now be excavated, at an increased expenditure of labour, in order, when coined into money, to buy the same quantity of goods, than was formerly necessary. The production of the raw metal has diminished, because the cost of extracting it from the mines which are closed is not covered by the value of the commodities for which it exchanges when used as money. Silver, and the remark applies in a greater degree to gold, cannot be indefinitely increased in quantity. These metals cannot be obtained with as much ease as copper or iron. There is a point which, in comparison with the case of the latter, is soon reached, at which the labour required for the excavation of a given quantity will not exchange for the same amount of labour bestowed on the acquisition of other commodities. The metals cost in fact more than they fetch; their cost prohibits their production; and however active the demand for them may be in stimulating mining enterprise by the hope of extraordinary profits, the rarity of the metals, especially gold, and the difficulty of extracting it from the earth, is frequently so great that the cost of its production cannot practically be surmounted. This condition operates to limit the quantity available for use as money, and necessarily prevents that quantity fluctuating in value against commodities to the same extent that commodities, which are capable of increase in more extended quantities than gold, fluctuate against one another. Thus, if there be two classes of mines, A and B, and from A the return to one day's labour is one hundred ounces of gold, and from B the return to ten days' labour is only the same quantity, the A class of miners will at first obtain for their one day's labour ten times the goods in exchange for their gold that the B class get. The continued increment of gold from the A mines will, the amount of commodities exchangeable for gold remaining the same, lower its value, and more and more gold will have to be given for the same quantity of goods. In this event, the time will come when the B class of miners will not find that the goods which they get for their gold on putting it into the market are of equal value to the labour bestowed on the excavation of the metal from their mines, and they will cease to work them in obedience to the law of the cost of production. As the difficulty of excavating gold from the B mines at a profit increased, the owners will have endeavoured to exchange their produce for as many commodities as possible, and this, to some extent, would save the A miners from the necessity of forcing a market for theirs by offering it in increasing quantities for the same quantity of goods, and the final expulsion of the gold of the B mines from the market would arrest the fall in the exchange value of the A gold. Furthermore, as the gold at first from both classes, and latterly from only one class of mines came into the market, it would find an equilibrium established between the existing stock of gold and commodities in general. It would take a long time for the fresh increments of gold to disturb the balance of values existing between gold and goods in the market, and as those who at each transaction in the exchange of the fresh gold for goods would seek to make a profit on exchanging the gold for a larger quantity of any commodity than they had given for it, increasing supplies of commodities would be offered for exchange against the fresh supplies of gold, and in this way also the exchange value of the whole mass of gold offered for all the goods in the market would not fall in value so fast as it might, under other circumstances. The maintenance of value, or the fluctuations in value of the gold, has now become regulated by the law of supply and demand. From the time that the gold was merged in the general circulation, its cost of production having been once covered, the question of its value in exchange for commodities became almost entirely one of quantity. So far as its cost of production affected its value, that consideration tended towards lowering it, because a large part of the quantity was produced at a much smaller expenditure of labour than that by which the rest of the gold in the market had been on the average obtained; but, at the same time, the demand for gold for use in exchanging commodities ranged so high that the owners of the new gold were able to get for it not much less, measured in labour, than the owners of the existing stock had up to that time procured. While, therefore, the cost of production ultimately regulates the value of the metal, as we have seen in the case of the B mines, the law of supply and demand immediately and directly fixes from time to time the exchange value of the gold as against commodities.

Money can never vary much in its value in exchange from the value imposed upon it by the cost of its production (in the sense previously indicated), since behind the money in use there is always found a stock of bullion, which its owners are waiting to put into circulation as coin, when by doing so they can get a price for it which will somewhat exceed that cost and yield them a fair profit.

So far as this cost may be a low rather than a high cost, or, in other words, to any extent to which the owners of bullion convert it into coin, in order to exchange it for a large rather than a small quantity of goods (the labour expended in the production of the gold being compared with that expended in the production of the goods), money will be supplied in correspondence with the high figure at which its exchange value can be maintained, and prices will continue during that time to be low.

Bullion, although it frequently and in individual cases is, on its conversion into coin, put into circulation at a loss, yet, on the average and in the long run, the whole mass of money it provides must either command its equivalent in goods on its first introduction among commercial exchanges, or it will cease to be excavated. The raw metal, in its latter and artificial character as money, becomes liable to an infinite variety of fluctations in correspondence with the varying proportions between the stock of money in use and the quantity of commodities which it serves to exchange. That is to say, that the exchange value of money depends immediately on the quantity of it and the work which that quantity has to do, and this is commonly described by the term, supply and demand. But as the volume of money which flows into the market depends on the greater or less advantage attending the conversion of bullion into coin, and that again on the cost of the production of the former, it follows that that cost is the consideration which ultimately and in the long run regulates the supply of coined money.

It must be understood that in this discussion by gold is meant gold money, since the principles which regulate the exchange value of money apply directly only to coined money in use, or reserved for immediate use. The potential influence of uncoined metal on the stock of money in use need not be considered in an argument which is intended to make clear the proposition, that the precious metals, when coined into money and allowed to circulate together without restriction on the quantity of either, exchange for one another on the basis of their relative intrinsic value, which itself is ultimately governed by the cost of their production.

LAW OF SUPPLY AND DEMAND.

The precious metals being, when coined into money, the most convenient vehicle for the transfer of goods in commerce from one owner to another, by doing that easily, surely, and quickly, which without their assistance could only be effected by the slow and uncertain method of barter, they have acquired a monopoly of employment as a medium of exchange; and although money, as has already been shown, is a commodity, this circumstance distinguishes it from other articles of commerce in a very essential manner. Of the metals ordinarily used as money, gold has, for the present, so far superseded every other, among European races, that it will be convenient to speak of gold alone in this place when using the term money. One incident of this monopoly is, that coined money, while it excludes all other articles from its own field of employment, is itself of no use anywhere else, of no use, that is to say, in a commercial sense.

The question of credit contrivances for minimising the use of metallic money need not now be considered, as they do not affect the principle under discussion.

It follows from this, that although the cost of

production of bullion may be reduced, that the value of money, using the term in the sense of efficiency for purchase, will not necessarily be diminished likewise. Gold bullion, if cheapened, will probably be used more extensively than before in the arts, and if a market is forced for its employment as money by a higher price being offered than before for the same article, the owners of the surplus stock of gold will either gain a smaller profit by employing it as money than they would gain by converting it into plate or jewellery, or the higher prices in money offered for commodities will bring into the market fresh supplies, and the previously existing equilibrium between money and goods will be restored. That which gives an increased value or purchasing power to money is an increase in the whole of the commodities which are under exchange for one another in the market, while the stock of money in use for their exchange remains the same.

It is not irrelevant to remark in this place that it is the proportion between commodities in exchange and money (to the exclusion of bullion) which exchange value depends upon. The presence of mere bullion in any country has only an indirect and prospective influence on the value of money, except it be itself under exchange among other commodities in the market, in the form of plate, ingots, or ornaments, in which case it increases the sum of those commodities which the money itself is being used to exchange, and by throwing more work on this stock of money, bullion, in this case, raises the exchange value of money and lowers prices.

If a reduction in the cost of bullion were to occur at a time when new methods for cheapening manufactures and produce were being invented and employed, more money would be coined ; but in that case commodities might be neither cheaper nor dearer. If, on the other hand, commodities were cheapened and offered for sale in increased quantities, and no more money were for any reason coined, the purchasing power of the money in use would be raised ; and the contrary would be the case if more money were issued while the quantity of commodities under exchange in the market remained the same.

But changes in the relative value of money and goods do not necessarily correspond with alterations in the cost of the production of money. Let us suppose that an equation of value exists between two tons of coal and one quarter of wheat, and that £2 serves to exchange them. If, owing to the cost of the production of money being lessened, more gold coin were brought into the market, £2 5s. might be the sum of money necessary to effect the exchange ; the value of money would have fallen, but the fall would not necessarily have been in the ratio of the cheapening of the cost of the production of money. Its value would have altered in accordance with the inclination or necessity of its owners to force a market for their money, but for which they might reserve their gold as bullion, and buy coals and wheat at the same price as before.

Again, in the case in which no diminution in the cost of producing money might take place, and the stock of money in the market were to remain unaltered, yet if a cessation in manufactures were simultaneously to occur, and the quantity of goods under exchange were to fall off, the purchasing power of money would diminish: £2 5s., instead of £2, might be required to buy the same quantity of coals or wheat; and this alteration would in no way correspond with a diminution in the cost of the production of money. The immediate, not the remote, cause of fluctuations in the purchasing power of money, that is, of prices rising or falling, is to be sought in the varying proportions which from time to time are found to occur between the amount of commodities under exchange and the amount of money in use for affecting the exchanges.

The exclusive function which money possesses as a medium of exchange invests it with properties peculiar to itself, which are not repeated in the same degree and manner in any other production of nature or art. While, as has been shown, its efficiency in exchange is ultimately regulated by the cost of its production, its value does not rise and fall week by week against that of commodities, in correspondence with variations in the cost of its production, nor does it remain steady at one point because its cost of production has not been affected in the same manner that commodities, the supply of which is replenished with ease, ordinarily rise and fall against one another. The cost of putting money in the market having been once covered, which must be assumed to be the case on its first appearance as coin, its purchasing power depends on the greater or less amount of work which commerce may put upon it. For this reason money has justly been compared to a machine, a locomotive engine, or a cart in use for exchanging the goods produced in one district with those of another. The cost of the engine having once been covered, its efficiency in use depends on whether it has one hundred or two hundred tons of material to drag. These machines may become cheaper, and more of them be brought into use, but they will not be more efficient for the whole work of haulage required of them, if the quantity of material for transportation is increased in consequence of their number. This same characteristic "e converso," makes money useless when it has been withdrawn from work and has been buried, as is often the case, in India. The potentiality of wealth may be to its owner a matter of pleasing reflection, but his money is as useless to him, in a technical sense, as when it lay buried as undiscovered metal in the mine.

Money being at once an equivalent and a measure of value, it is only of use when put to work as a machine for effecting exchanges, and in this respect it differs from most commodities, which are best employed when they are being consumed, and are of least use in exchanging other things; but those qualities which invest money with its function to exchange other things, at the same time bring it within the scope of the law of the cost of its production, and of the law of supply and demand in the same manner, although under more complicated conditions than those by which other productions of nature and human labour are affected.

The principal factor regulating the action of supply and demand is the necessity or inclination of the purchaser, and this is equally true of money and of goods. If an article cost only £1 to produce, it will, nevertheless, fetch £2 if purchasers are able and willing to pay that price for it; but when the supply reaches a point at which the demand ceases to induce increased production, the law of the cost of production comes into play. Where, however, the line can be drawn which separates the action of either principle, nothing but experience can in each case determine. If the cost of production were a constant quantity, this might often be possible. In the case, however, of most productions of nature, the cost of adapting them to men's purposes is but little less variable than the demand for them.

The variations in the relative value of commodities to one another from week to week are beyond measure numerous and diversified, and they depend on circumstances which are constantly changing. Among these, not the least important are fashion, caprice, and other motives which are included in the desire of acquisition. The force, therefore, of these influences, and the origin of these variations in most cases baffle investigation. The daily experience of those who succeed in business in proportion to the accuracy of their observation is the only gauge of the alternate depressions and elevations of value which occur among different kinds of commodities in respect to one another, and of money in relation to all articles offered for sale.

The law of the cost of production and the law of supply and demand are both at work together, and each contributes to settle the respective values of different merchants' wares; but we can no more state with certainty the influence of either factor on the resulting price than we can say whether three or two in a multiplication sum have most to do with making six. That the cost of production must be met on an average of transactions in any particular class of produce, or the article will cease to be produced, is at least certain, but since in regard to objects of luxury and many of necessity, the price, after the cost of production is covered, depends largely on the relative force of two mental conceptions, the desire of acquisition on the one hand, and a reluctance to give up the fruit of labour until its utmost value is ascertained on the other, and these involve a great variety of complex and associated motives, their ratio to one another cannot be stated in other terms than those of the money employed in the exchange. These terms, being always used in a relative sense, have no meaning sufficiently fixed to be capable of expression in terms, as definite as those used, for instance, in arithmetic. Thus, although the shares in a coal mine may have cost ten years ago £2 apiece, and to-day sell for £10, yet we cannot with so much certainty affirm that the scrip has become five times as valuable as before, as we can that twice five makes ten, because it is not at once ascertainable what influences have been at work to cause this alteration in price. If the coal selling for £10 only procures the same amount and kind of goods which ten years before cost £2, the coal has not risen in value, although it may sell for more money.

BIMETALLISM AND THE FIXED RATIO.

The effort to establish by law a fixed ratio of value between gold and silver money, at which either kind of coin shall be used indifferently as legal payment of debts, and which shall never be disturbed by the interference of the natural ratio of value subsisting between them has failed; for one reason among others that in Asia there exists a continual and insatiable demand for gold, and a silver treasure of vast dimensions which would be employed in buying up the undervalued gold circulating in the currencies of Europe at the arbitrary rate of 15½ ozs. of silver in exchange for 1 oz. of gold (instead of at about 18 ozs. of silver, which is the natural and market value of the latter metal) as fast as it were coined and put into circulation. The bimetallists hope that if all gold-using nations agree to use silver in their currencies at a rate of exchange of 1 : 15½, that 1 oz. of gold, which is now worth 18 ozs. of silver, will fall to a valuation of 15½ ozs. This result, they believe, will follow from their fixing the exchange value of gold and silver money at the figure above stated. In effect they argue thus, that the legal rate of exchange will govern the market for gold and silver; that if the civilized world can, by international agreement, make the gold and silver money of their currencies exchange on these terms, then bullion dealers, miners, and the inhabitants of semi-civilized countries, who use in their currencies *more than one-half of all the silver coin in the world*, and possess besides a great treasure of silver bullion, will likewise exchange gold and silver at the same rate. To these speculative economists the question may be put, Why should they? This question must be answered before the possibility of such a contingency can be admitted.

If it were one of the results of a fixation of value for gold at 1 oz. for 15½ ozs. of silver, that silver were brought to the mints of the gold-using countries in such large quantities for coinage, that very little remained available for sale or use elsewhere, no doubt silver would rise in value to the level fixed by the Convention; but it is evident that this can only occur at the cost of the gold coin of those currencies into which the silver would be coined. The new silver would, in fact, be brought in excessive quantities, and coined into money solely with the object of buying the gold out of those currencies and taking it to the East, where it would be used to purchase 20 per cent. more silver than that with which the gold had itself been bought. The new silver would, in fact, be substituted for the old gold, and the currencies of mixed gold and silver would be converted into mono-metallic silver currencies.*

The amount of metal now current in countries using both gold and silver is probably not less than is sufficient for the work it has to do: there may be in some currencies too little gold, and in others too little silver for perfect convenience, but no great and sudden addition to these currencies can be made, unless there occurs a correspondingly great and sudden increase to the commodities brought to market for exchange with one another, by means of the coined money in circulation. It follows, therefore, that if any quantity of silver, much in excess of that now in use, is coined into the currencies of gold-using countries, it can only get into circulation by expelling an equivalent value of the gold coin. In any view of the case, therefore, the fixation of a rate of exchange at 1 : 15½ would defeat its own object; either the new silver would expel the gold from circulation, or, if it were coined and not used

* The reader will excuse the employment of arguments that the author has more than once published on this subject.—C. D.

as money, would remain surplus silver still. Its market value would not be regulated by the rate of exchange fixed by law. The owners of stocks of silver would not hold them in the vain expectation of buying gold at the rate of 1 oz. for 15½ ozs. of silver, but would seek to realize the ordinary profits of their business, by selling the metal at its market value in gold—18 ozs., or whatever it might be. The inhabitants of Asia and other silver-using regions of the globe would continue to exchange their gold and silver at its natural ratio of value, uninfluenced by the law of the bimetallic Convention, and as fast as they spent their stock of silver in buying the undervalued gold coin of the Western nations, they would procure fresh supplies of silver at a price which, though lower than 15½ ozs. for 1 oz. of gold, would yet yield a profit on the mining of silver, and repeat the operation.

No possible stimulus to the use of silver as coin, which the bimetallic ratio can provide, will cause the absorption of so large a portion of the metal easily obtainable for conversion into coin as to invest the remainder with a value which is about 20 per cent. higher than it is reckoned at in the market, since whatever the quantity may be which would be coined into the currencies of bimetallic countries, its place will be immediately taken by fresh silver excavated from the earth at a cost so low as to be fatal to the maintenance of the arbitrary ratio of value, which the bimetallic Convention seeks to establish.

The fixation of a rate of exchange for coined gold and silver money as a means of raising the market value of silver in gold, or as a method for working a mixed currency, in which either metal may be used in unlimited quantities, can only result in failure. The cause of failure is to be found in the departure, which such a system makes, from the only true principle upon which gold and silver can be made to circulate together, in quantities regulated solely by the volition of the people using the currency, viz. that of the exchange of the coins on the basis of their intrinsic value.

The scheme for fixing the exchange value of money by law at an unalterable ratio ignores those fundamental laws which govern the use of money in trade. A deliberate violation of principles which are true to the natural order of human affairs in finance, as in morals, involves conditions of failure which, if for a time their influence is suppressed, will ultimately make themselves felt; and the retribution exacted will be out of all proportion more grievous than the original inconvenience. But it is not likely that any serious attempt will be made to enforce such a system. The more it is examined the more apparent is its radical unsoundness, and objections, which may almost be called physical objections, to its practical application arise, which are seen to be insuperable.

Ratio of Gold to Silver in the East and West compared.

The relative value of gold and silver prevailing in the East during the Middle Ages is evidence that the principles above discussed are those upon which the exchange value of money rests, when its circulation is free, and the coins exchange at their natural value in one another. In the East this has always been the case. Token-money, or money circulating at a conventional valuation, was unknown until the era of the English rule; and in the Indian currency, copper coin and paper money corresponding to the bank note of England alone circulate on such terms.

Japan was, at the time of its discovery by the Portuguese in 1545, entirely secluded from the Western world, and apparently carried on but little commerce with its nearest neighbour, China. Mines in the islands supplied its people with such quantities of gold and silver as they required for all purposes. The ratio of value at that date was, in Japan, one of gold to six of silver. Under these circumstances, it is probable that the ratio of value between gold and silver money depended almost entirely on the relative cost of the production of either. From what is known of Japan at the first visit which Europeans paid to the islands, it may be inferred that the trade customs of its inhabitants were even of a more primitive description than those prevailing in Europe at the same time. There was but little public revenue raised in money. Public and private services were paid for by assignments of land or produce. The Japanese had no foreign commerce at all. Very little coin of either kind could have been in demand.

During the next eighty years the Portuguese, by selling Japanese productions at an enormous profit in China and Europe, and exchanging their silver for Japanese gold, which in Spain and England was rated at that time at from $1 : 10\frac{3}{4}$ to $1 : 11\frac{1}{20}$, brought the Japanese ratio under the influence of the stocks of gold existing in other parts of the East and in the West, and the value of gold as against silver rose to at least 1 : 10, and is stated to have risen higher. In 1624, the Portuguese were banished from the Japanese islands, and the Dutch trade placed under restrictions, which protected the currency of the country from foreign influences, and the ratio fell, according to information quoted by Del Mar, to its former figure of 1 : 6 or 7. Sir Rutherford Alcock ("Japan," vol. i., p. 281) states that at the opening of the ports to British commerce in 1859, the ratio was 1 : 3. Having regard to the large amount of gold exported by the Portuguese and Dutch between 1545 and 1706, estimated by Del Mar at £35,000,000, and to the fact that it was derived from sources which probably did not yield increased supplies in correspondence with the withdrawal of this treasure, the latter of these two ratios seems likely to be the more correct. The ratio of value was influenced during the period that Japanese money was employed in foreign commerce by the action of supply and demand. When it ceased to be so used, the law of the cost of its production seems again to have asserted its ascendancy.

So in China, the ratio at the end of the sixteenth century was 1 : 10; while in Europe, which was then beginning to feel the influence of the importations of American silver, it stood at 1 : 12. Silver and gold, which are indigenous in China, would necessarily find their way there from Europe only in small quantities, and both the action of trade and the somewhat indirect courses in which it was carried on with China would not tend to induce speedy or large importations of either metal into that country. As late as 1776 the ratio was said to have been only 1 : 12, while in England it stood at 1 : $15\frac{1}{5}$ at nearly the same time.

In Europe, on the other hand, which was earliest exposed to the influx of the newly discovered silver from America, and especially in Spain, the Netherlands, and England, which were the first countries to appropriate this treasure, the ratio varied under the alternating pressure of the cost of the production of the new metal and of the demand for it, which arose with the renascence of the commercial spirit in Western Europe during the reigns of Henry VIII. and Elizabeth.

The effect of the American treasure on the stocks of the precious metals in Europe was not complete until the beginning of the eighteenth century. During the earlier years of Queen Elizabeth's reign (*circa* 1560), the ratio of gold to silver was 1 : $11\frac{15}{70}$. In 1600, the ratio calculated at the mint prices for standard gold and silver was 1 : 11. In 1604 (2 King James I.), it had risen to exactly 1 : 12; and in 1717 (3 King George I.), to 1 : $15\frac{9}{124}$.*

The "Treatise on the Coins" informs us that

* The ratios which Lord Liverpool gives in his "Treatise on the Coins" are somewhat higher than these, which are calculated from MacCulloch's tables, and the Silver Committee's Report, 1876.

during the sixty years following the accession of King James I., silver fell in the gold valuation 32 per cent., and by the second year of King George I. it had fallen 39 per cent. on its value one hundred and fifteen years before.

The earliest record we have of the ratio of value between these metals in India is connected with the subjection of Phœnicia by Darius, B.C. 517. The conqueror required the Tyrian tribute to be paid in silver, which in Persia was $\frac{1}{13}$ of the value of gold, while in India it was $\frac{1}{4}$; and thus obtained for the Persians the advantage of exchanging this silver for gold in their Indian trade, which the Tyrians might have secured for themselves if they had paid the Persian king in gold procured from that country in exchange for their silver, and at the same time have lightened the burden of their tribute.

That the ratio fell as increasing quantities of Spanish and Grecian silver in ancient times, of silver from Hungarian and other European mines in the Middle Ages, and American silver from the beginning of the sixteenth century onwards, arrived in India, cannot be doubted. Our information on this subject is somewhat obscure, but as the ratio of value between the two metals in pre-Christian times recorded in such reliable historical accounts as have come down to us is found to have ranged in Europe between

1 : 10 and 1 : 12, and to have remained at about that value for the first fifteen centuries of our era—allowance being made for abnormal perturbations attributable to transitory and local causes—it is safe to infer that the variations in the relative value of the two metals which existed on either side of the known world were progressively becoming less, and gold and silver in India gradually approaching the same value as against each other that they held in Europe and Western Asia.

The principles previously discussed which govern the exchange value of money involve this conclusion. If the price of a commodity is high in one part of the world, people who export goods to that quarter will increase their exportations, in order to get a larger share of the redundant money circulating there, and by bringing it home exchange it for goods costing more labour than those they had exported. High prices in one of two countries trading together, and low prices in another, indicate a difference of level which is sooner or later rectified by the export of produce to the dearer or the import of money into the cheaper country, or by both means. The price of commodities tends to seek the level of common cost of production, and it has been shown that money in a condition of absolutely free coinage and circulation in the long run exchanges against commodities on the basis of the cost of the production of both. This being the case, the money of two countries trading together, *is in respect of the commodities which they exchange*, always approximating to the character of a common measure of value. Indian gold money will be of much the same efficiency to purchase indigo in India, as English gold money is in England for the same purpose. English gold money will not go much farther in purchasing iron in England than Indian gold will in the purchase of English iron in India, the difference being the amount of profit required by the trader in either case. As when two kinds of money are in free circulation together they exchange on the basis of their intrinsic value, the ratio of value between them obeys the same law, as the ratio of value existing between either of them and commodities in commerce. It follows as a necessary consequence that the use of both metals as a common measure of value in effecting the exchange of commodities in commerce always exerts an equalizing influence on the relation which they bear to one another over the whole area of their employment. This inference agrees with the facts of the case.

Mr. Keene* has found it recorded in the "Aieen

* Author of "The Moghul Empire," and other critical and historical essays on Indian subjects.

Akbari," that in the Emperor Akbar's reign (*circa* 1590) a gold coin weighing 91 tolahs 8 maashas (*i.e.* 1100 m.) was equal in value to 100 round gold mohurs, each of which was worth 9 rupees, and weighed 11 maashas (*i.e.* $\frac{11}{12}$ of a tolah). The ratio obtaining between gold and silver on these terms was 1 : $9\frac{9}{11}$, assuming that the silver rupee weighed a full tolah, which was likely to be the case, as at that period a rupee and a tolah were names indifferently used for the same weight. As in England in 1600, the ratio was 1 : 11, the difference to a purchaser buying a pound of silver with gold would have been $1\frac{2}{11}$ lbs. in favour of his doing so in England rather than in India, and this proves that up to that time gold had been accumulating in India rather than silver, while the contrary had been the case in Europe.

The cost of transporting silver from Europe and coining it in India (a seignorage being charged in the British mints in that country) is calculated to have amounted at the end of the last century to 8 per cent., and it is not likely to have been less one hundred years previous, but at the same time 2 or 3 per cent. may be deducted, as it is not certain what seignorage, if any, was levied for coinage at the numerous mints of the native princes, from which coin was issued. If to 108 tolahs (the weight of silver in 9 rupees) is added 6 per cent. for the cost of transportation, then the value of this quantity of the metal would be to the importer 114 rupees (or tolahs) 7 anas and 8 pies; and if 5 per cent. were added, Rs. 113 6 a. 4 p.; the former giving a ratio of 1 : $10\frac{13}{32}$, and the latter a ratio of 1 : $10\frac{15}{192}$, while, as has been seen, the ratio stood at 1 : 11 in England at about the same date (1600).

On the other hand, if the cost of importing gold to India were 5 or 6 per cent. on its value, a piece of gold sufficient to make one of these round gold mohurs, weighing 11 maashas, would, on its arrival, for the purposes of the importer's business, take a ratio to the silver in the country of 1 : $9\frac{27}{77}$ if 5 per cent. were the cost of transportation, and a ratio of 1 : $9\frac{153}{583}$ if 6 per cent. were the cost.

More than a hundred years later, Sir Isaac Newton, who was Master of the Royal Mint, and is not likely to have been wrong, stated in the year 1717 that "in the East Indies a pound weight of fine gold may be worth twelve pounds of fine silver," while in England it was worth $15\frac{9}{124}$ pounds of silver.

The diffusion of the American silver had evidently reached India by the beginning of the eighteenth century, but the existing stocks of gold which we have seen to have been in process of accumulation during many centuries, were still sufficiently large to give silver a higher value as against gold in India than in England, and to act as an encouragement to the exportation of silver from the West to the East.

In Bengal, a gold mohur was issued by the Indian Government in 1769, and ordered to pass as legal tender payment for 16 sicca rupees. The intrinsic value of this coin was estimated to be equal to the nominal value of it, or as nearly so as was deemed necessary to render it current at the prescribed rate; but from causes arising out of the state of confusion which then prevailed in the Indian currencies, its circulation was confined during the next twenty years almost entirely to Calcutta. It was no doubt overvalued in silver at the Indian rate of valuation, as it was bought up by persons making payments to Government, and used for that purpose in preference to the silver coin. The ratio of value thus set up between the pure gold in this mohur and the pure silver in the sicca rupee was about $1 : 15\frac{1}{17}$.

The prevailing ratio in the north of Europe about the year 1770 was $1 : 14\frac{3}{4}$. In 1793, a new gold mohur and a new rupee were struck, the former of which was directed to pass for sixteen of the latter. As the gold mohur contained $189\frac{463}{1000}$ grs. of pure gold, and the rupee contained $175\frac{231}{250}$ grs. of pure silver, the ratio obtaining between the coins was $1 : 14\frac{43}{50}$. In Europe the ratio at the same date was $1 : 15\frac{21}{50}$. In

1818, another gold mohur and another rupee were issued, the ratio of value between these coins was almost exactly 1 : 15, while in Europe the ratio was 1 : $15\frac{51}{100}$. A slight alteration was made in the value of the rupee in 1833, which need not be noticed here, as two years later the currency of the East India Company's territories was remodelled and placed on its present footing.

By reason of the superiority of value which silver in India enjoyed over the same metal in England inducing its importation into the former country, a preference would be given to gold when a necessity arose of exporting either metal from India. As, however, the profits of traders depended on the sale in Europe of Indian commodities, and the latter ordinarily exceeded in value the goods sent in exchange, gold must necessarily have been taken from India to Europe in but small quantities. The approximation of the ratios of value prevailing in both countries to one another, depending principally on an increase in the stock of silver in the East, was only gradually effected, and its completion was more definitely declared than at any previous time when the Indian silver coinage was put on its present footing, and gold demonetised in 1835.

It has been estimated that, up to the end of the eighteenth century, gold to the value of £100,000,000 sterling was sent from the West to the East, *i.e.* to India, Malacca, the Straits, and China. After making a fair deduction for such withdrawals of gold from India as resulted from the sack of Delhi by Nadir Shah in 1738, and for other occasions on which gold obtained by plunder in the East has found its way back to Europe, a balance of from £80,000,000 to £90,000,000 must have remained in those islands and countries. The course of trade for centuries carried gold to continental India and Ceylon in much larger quantities than to any other country still further east, and of this estimated sum of £80,000,000 or £90,000,000, £60,000,000 or £70,000,000 may fairly be credited as the share which India herself appropriated and retained. To this must be added the proceeds of her own mines, and gold obtained by trade from Central Asia, China, Burmah, Siam, and other Asiatic sources. The sources of gold supply in Asia itself were in all probability more fertile than those situated in Arabia, Africa, Asia Minor, or Greece, and were more accessible to the Indians. The ancient books of that people, and occasional notices of their country in classical writers, refer to their wealth (which in those days meant stores of the precious metals) as exceeding that of western nations. If, therefore, so large a treasure as £60,000,000 of gold was taken from the West to India previous to the nineteenth century, it is by no means extravagant to estimate the treasure drawn by India from Eastern Asia at £40,000,000 more.

Looking also to the necessities of her people, their industrious habits, the shrewd and enterprising spirit of the trading classes, their numerous cities and towns, the density of the population, the variety of their occupations and amusements, the large armies maintained by their rulers, and the comparatively high degree of organization which their political and social system had attained to, we find all those conditions united in India, which in all other countries are accompanied with a plentiful use of coined money. This estimate of £100,000,000 of gold as the treasure existing in India at the beginning of the nineteenth century is therefore, probably, much below the mark.

From the year 1835 onwards, we have reliable statistics compiled by the Indian Government of the movement of the precious metals to and from India. Accounts brought up to April, 1882, show that there has been imported into India, *and never been re-exported*, a gold treasure which is valued in the returns at upwards of £112,000,000. If this is added to the estimate compiled on the facts and arguments in the preceding observations of the stock of gold existing in India at the end of the last century, the country must contain a treasure which probably exceeds £212,000,000 in value, or* about two and a half times the amount of gold which is believed to be in circulation in the United Kingdom.

GOLD COIN FORMERLY CURRENT IN INDIA.

General Ballard, the late Master of the Bombay Mint, writing in 1868 of the stock of gold bullion in India, remarks "If no mints existed, it would be worth while building them on the chance of coining a fraction of this immense treasure; but the mints exist. It is only the mint rules which require alteration to allow of our solving the problem, whether there is any desire on the part of the owners of this bullion to have a portion of it converted into coined money." The authors of the recently published work "Finances and Public Works of India," after describing the introduction of the present silver currency of India in the year 1835, and the demonetization of gold, speak of the gold mohur, which is occasionally coined in the Indian mints. It contains exactly as many grains of fine gold as the rupee contains grains of fine silver, but, as by law it is not legal

* From £80,000,000 to £90,000,000.

tender, it is rarely seen. The writers go on to say, that "the opinion has been expressed that gold money is not used in India because the people prefer silver by reason of the small amount of their transactions. There is, however, no real evidence of this, the fact being that for three quarters of a century at least gold coin has either not been legal tender or has been improperly valued, so that either it could not come into circulation or could not remain in circulation in competition with the silver rupee which has always been the standard coin. Towards the end of the last century, gold coins circulated freely with silver in most parts of Bengal, and about half the revenue was paid in gold. Forty years ago, gold coins were still to be found in use in some of the districts of Madras. Gold, however, everywhere gradually went out of circulation, and for a great many years has, for all practical purposes, ceased to be employed as money. At various times gold coins have been received in payment of government demands, at varying rates, but under the law of 1835 they ceased to be legal tender." *

The difficulty which the East India Company's governors found, at the end of the last and the beginning of the present century, in ascertaining the relative value of gold and silver coin, arose from

* Pages 381, 382.

the multiplicity of currencies in use, which are stated to have been as many as forty throughout the country; from the difficulty of communication, which while it hindered an equalization of the values of commodities in distant places had indirectly a similar effect on the gold and silver coin in use; from the comparatively scanty supply of coin; from the small influence of the bullion market of the West on that of India, and from the length of time it took for that influence to be exerted in days when a voyage to the East from Europe was of six months' duration. All these conditions are in the present day exactly reversed. Only one currency is used in India, with which at least the British Government need concern itself. The relative value of gold and silver money at Calcutta would act in a day on the valuation at Lahore and Bombay. Coin is more abundant, and its efficiency in the exchange with England, which is now for such purposes within momentary reach of India, can be ascertained daily, or hourly if necessary. The argument that in a bygone period (from ninety to one hundred years ago) the intrinsic value in one another of the gold and silver money of India could not be accurately ascertained, is of no force now, when every circumstance which bears on that valuation combines to make it both certain and notorious.

PART II.

Desire of People of India for Gold Coin.

Those who are acquainted with the facts know that a gold currency would be highly acceptable to the richer class of people in India. The Currency Commission reported * "that the demand for gold currency is unanimous throughout the country."

Gold coins of the Emperor Akbar's currency (1555–1605) are imitated and used for hoarding or reserve by bankers, as they have a recognized value in the Indian bullion market. In 1870, when the rupee began to fall in value, several lacs of rupees' worth of gold ornaments were brought to the Bombay mint in a few months for assay and conversion into bars, in order to be exported for the purchase of silver. No considerable banker is without a hoard of gold in coin or in the small blocks cast in a mould, as a support to his commercial credit. People of wealth who are not engaged in trade, are commonly possessed of a store of gold treasure, the existence of which appears to be no secret in the case of some conspicuous persons.

* Printed for Parliament, 16th of March, 1868, para. 4.

Coins are hoarded in preference to ornaments, as their value is more certain, and the seller generally loses, both on converting bullion into ornaments or when selling them for silver. The manufacturer takes his profit in the one case; and in the other, the assayer and purchaser are generally the same person. The sovereigns of the Royal and of the Australian Mints are to be bought in every large town in the country, and are daily quoted in the exchange tables published at the capitals. The amount of these coins in India may probably be numbered by the million. Sovereigns can be said to circulate in India in the sense that they daily change owners. The gold mohur, on the other hand, which is occasionally coined by the Indian Government, is so rarely seen as to be a curiosity. In times of pressure, French, Turkish, American, and Russian gold coins are brought to the mints to be melted and assayed. The Italian sequin, which came into India with the European trade of the Middle Ages, is obtainable without much difficulty in many parts of the country, and is believed to be extensively imitated and sold from its value being well known to the class of people who keep gold in store. Such men have no difficulty in discriminating between the different qualities of gold in the market, and fixing the relative value which one description holds towards another. For most uses to which gold may be put in India, it will be more useful in the form of coin than in any other, and in the form of the £1 sterling of the realm more useful than if converted into any other kind of coin; because the certainty of its present value and its future stability as against silver and other commodities is more assured than if the metal were cast in any other shape. There can be no doubt that, when the state of the market makes it profitable to do so, the natives of India export gold to buy silver abroad for coinage into their own currency, and that, in like manner, the gold imported into India is partly used to purchase silver in India—one hoard being substituted for the other—which is then converted into coin. Gold is hoarded in preference to silver, for the reason already given, and because it cannot be employed as coin. If the mints were open to the coinage of an Indian sovereign, and it were made legal tender, neither of these operations would be necessary, and the sovereigns, if hoarded, would be immediately available when required for use in trade. But the currency policy of the Indian administration at present forbids the people to use their gold as coin in their own country.

In the arguments which follow, an attempt will be made to prove that gold can be introduced and circulated in the currency of India as legal tender coin at no greater cost to the State than the fabrication of the coins, a matter of a few shillings for every hundred pieces.*

PLAN FOR CIRCULATING GOLD MONEY.

The first question that will be asked is, How is a gold currency to be established in the Indian Empire? As an answer to this inquiry, the following plan is suggested.

(1) That the Government of India shall coin a gold coin in all respects identical with the £1 sterling of the currency of the realm, out of the stock of gold now to be found in India, to any amount, in which the metal may be brought by its owners to the mints for that purpose.

(2) That these gold coins shall be declared *legal tender* for the payment of *any sum of money due to*

* What this may amount to, depends on the way the calculation is made. If the mere cost of assaying, melting, and coining is considered, it would be very trifling, but would rise and fall as a smaller or greater number of coins might be struck at one time. If to the coinage of gold is attributed a part of the permanent expenses of the mint establishment, salaries, repairs of buildings, renewals of machinery, etc., on the *ad valorem* basis, the cost might be estimated at 2 per cent. or more when work was slack.

the Government of India, at the option of the party making the payment; and in other cases that they should be legal tender for the discharge of any obligation *amounting to* Rs. 5000 and upwards, at the *option of the party making the payment.*

(3) That the Government of India shall from time to time declare (but not more frequently than may be necessary and convenient) the rate at which the gold coin of its currency shall be accepted as legal payment of sums contracted to be paid in silver coin; and this State rate of conversion shall be strictly regulated by the market value of the silver rupees of the British Indian currency in these gold sovereigns.

(4) That the silver rupee shall still continue to be legal tender for all kinds of payments, and in any amount, at the option of the party making the payment.

(5) That no person (the Government excepted) shall be obliged to take payment in gold of a debt due to be paid in silver, which may be less in amount than Rs. 5000, unless he shall previously have agreed with his debtor to do so.

Argument for First Proposal.

The inducements to the owners of gold to bring it for coinage to the mints are those which have induced every nation, as its trade, both external and internal, expands, to prefer gold to any other metal for the settlement of large transactions. Its efficiency as a purchasing agent is more steady than that of silver, and therefore profits to be made on purchases paid for in gold are calculable with more certainty over long periods of time than when they are effected with the latter metal. The £1 sterling of the United Kingdom is a recognized standard of value in every country with which India has trade dealings. It is the single isobare by which an equilibrium of value between different commodities in widely separated regions of the globe can be quickly and surely ascertained. To endow India with a gold currency is to give her people, and those they trade with in foreign countries, a new and efficient implement for exchanging productions, to make a valuable improvement in the machinery of commerce. Politically, such a measure would tend to bind by a fresh chain the interests of England and her Dependency; it would be a distinct step towards making the two countries commercially one. To the objection that what a man can buy with gold he can equally well buy with an equivalent value of silver, it is a sufficient answer to point to the history of the coins of the realm, and of the currencies of the civilized world in modern times, of France, Germany, Italy, and the United States of America. This teaches us that the use of gold, as the standard of value, is the only expedient for eliminating the risks and uncertainties in which commerce is involved when conducted exclusively with silver as a medium of exchange. Various as the reasons may be why traders during two centuries have gradually substituted gold for silver as the basis of their transactions with foreigners, they all point to one conclusion, that the metal which experience proves to be most advantageous for mercantile purposes in the rest of the world will be of equal convenience in the Indian trade. It is too obvious to require argument for its proof that if the jute and indigo of the Calcutta market can be bought by the London merchant with gold current in that city, and exchanged somewhere else against another commodity on a gold valuation, an impulse would be given to the sale of the productions of India, which is to be measured by the ease and diminution of risk with which they are practically exchanged for the goods of the last country which receives them, and the market for their sale is actually enlarged by the Indian ryot being brought into more direct communication with purchasers residing in the most distant parts of the earth. It is equally opposed to reason and experience to assert, in respect of a trade which embraces the whole world, that it is of no importance at all that the nations engaged therein should possess a single measure for the value of the commodities which they offer for sale to one another, and one equivalent with which they can all alike exchange the goods they traffic in; that it is preferable to use two, one of which is itself but a commodity having a variable value and a tendency to become gradually but constantly less efficient as a purchasing agent. If the gold of India were coined in a form identical with the sovereign of the English currency, and were to circulate as legal tender coin, the Indian trader is far too keen not to perceive the advantage he would gain by bringing his hoard of gold to the mint and converting it into money, which would open to him more widely than is now possible the markets of the West, and allow him to buy and sell in Europe and America with one and the same coin, and with as much ease as in all parts of his own country.

If, at the same time, means were taken to attract part of the gold supply of India to the Indian mints in preference to that furnished by Australia and California, every thousand sovereigns so coined would be a clear addition to the stock of gold available for the world's use. This might be effected by issuing the coin to persons depositing gold at the mint free of any charge, except such as is made at the royal mint at the Tower on the fabrication of sovereigns. By this means, gold imported from Europe, Australia, or America, would be at a slight disadvantage to that which is now held in India; and as the latter would be exposed to no competition at the mint, and the public would be guaranteed against any charge but a very small seigniorage on the conversion of their gold into coin, it may reasonably be expected that the metal would be brought to the mint in just such quantities as could be profitably used as current coin in the trade; and this result is all that is sought or need be attained by any plan for introducing a gold currency into India.

The sole cost of the measure would be that incurred in the assay of the metal and its fabrication into sovereigns. As the Indian mints are inferior to none in the world for completeness and perfection of machinery, the expense incurred should not be greater than that of coining sovereigns in London, a very trifling price for the public to pay for so great a benefit as a gold currency.

By coining the proposed Indian sovereigns on exactly the same terms as those of the Royal currency, their reduction into bullion would be discouraged; and as their exportation as coin to foreign countries would in no way be restricted, they would be as efficient for all purposes of trade as English or Australian coins. It is of importance to encourage rather than otherwise the exportation of sovereigns of the Indian currency. The principles of free trade apply to the exchange of coined money as fully as they apply to the exchange of commodities, and to the interests of India their observance in this particular case is of essential importance, because the efficiency of the new gold coins, in a currency system under which they would exchange on the basis of their intrinsic value against the silver coins with which the bulk of the internal commerce of India is carried on, depends on their easily finding their actual level of value, when measured in the gold coin of foreign countries as well as in the silver money, and the productions of India itself. The exportation of the gold coin of India should be free. In the course of trade the exported coins will return home again, or their place be taken by sovereigns of the royal or colonial mints, which, from their being of exactly the same intrinsic value as the Indian coins, will be equally acceptable to the Indian trader, and therefore circulate as current money in the same way that Australian sovereigns circulate in London.

Argument for Second Proposal.

It would, however, be to no purpose that gold sovereigns were issued to the public from the Indian mints, except they were at the same time made legal tender for currency purposes in the country itself. It is for this reason that the gold mohur of the Indian Government is but seldom coined and never used as money. These coins if brought to the mint would be treated as bullion, and re-issued as legal tender sovereigns.

The £1 sterling of the Indian mint it is proposed to make legal tender coin of the currency of the country in all cases in which payment has to be made to the State, if the payer choose to use gold. In cases in which private persons or commercial companies shall agree by advertisement or otherwise to take small payments in sovereigns rather than in rupees.

In all cases in which a payment has to be made of Rs. 5000, or more.

In all cases the payment of sovereigns will be at the option of the person making the payment, if he prefer to pay in gold rather than in silver coin, and such a payment would legally discharge a debt.

It is needless to prove that no coin can become current as money except in so far as it is made legal tender for the payment of debts. This is not merely a theoretical but is an actual impediment to the use of gold at present, and if this were removed, the writer of these pages has reason to know that the native bankers in India would have no objection to use the new coins because they are gold rather than silver in their business.

If the Indian Government is by law bound to take its own sovereigns in liquidation of its own claims, confidence is at once given to the natives of the country to accept them; and as the same coins would always be readily taken by private persons in payments made by Government, a circulation of these coins in the bazaars would be set up and maintained. Private persons and trading companies might be given a legal power to declare payments in gold of small amounts to be valid payments of debts due to them. The railway and shipping companies, and probably many other firms and individuals engaged in business, would find it highly profitable to them to get payment of their receipts in gold coin, instead of in silver coin eighteen or twenty times the weight in metal, and so save risk and expense in bringing their revenues together at the head offices of their business. This is a consideration of no small importance in a country where the centres of trade and administration are separated from their subordinate agencies by distances measured in thousands of miles. Professional men would soon claim to be paid their fees in sovereigns, and shops conducted on ready-money principles would probably give a material preference to payments made by their customers in gold over those made in silver.

It is, however, necessary that the use of gold in small sums should in no cases be made obligatory, otherwise payments in gold might be demanded from people who would be unable to procure, or might not have sovereigns in their possession, from the character of their business being of a kind which is usually and more conveniently carried on with silver. Again, as will be seen from what follows, the number of rupees which may be the equivalent of a gold payment will vary from time to time. To take a small sum by way of example. If Rs. 12 at one time and Rs. 12¼ at another are the equivalent of a sovereign, to the uninstructed mind of the native of India a payment with a sovereign at one time may appear to be a smaller payment than when made at another, although the amount of food purchasable with the sovereign may on both occasions be the same. To avoid any chance of the use of the sovereigns becoming unpopular from this apparent variation in their value at the market, it is better to take no steps to introduce their circulation into the *petty* commerce of the country by law. The gold coins will, in the course of time, find their way into all markets, where they can be profitably used by the mere volition of the people themselves. There may be, and probably will be for sometime to come, in out-of-the-way places, a dislike to the use of the new gold coins, from the people being habituated to the use of silver rupees. From the fact that in such localities gold has not in this generation been seen in competition with silver, the traders who regulate the retail prices of commodities will, if their customers are required by law to use gold for making small payments, take advantage of their ignorance to defraud them.

None of these objections, however, apply to large transactions, involving single payments of Rs. 5000 and upwards. These are conducted on both sides by men of experience, engaged in a large way of business, who are not at all liable to be deceived, and are quite capable of looking after their own interests, and will take care to exact full legal payment in gold in lieu of the silver value of their goods. The use of gold coin is advocated principally in the interests of the foreign trade of India with gold-using countries, in which transactions of a lower value than Rs. 5000 are probably not common. An English merchant paying for Indian commodities would, therefore, be generally able to deal with the Indian vendor in the same coin that he would use if he were buying goods in London —the Indian being the intrinsic equivalent of the English sovereign. It will not be overlooked that, under this scheme, if the party making the payment choose, he is always at liberty to pay in silver coin instead of gold ; and, on the other hand, a vendor can always protect himself from a real or imaginary risk of loss in being required to take payment for Rs. 5000 in gold coin by drawing his contract to sell in terms of the gold instead of the silver currency. As a matter of fact there can be no doubt that in large trading cities, and for large transactions in all parts of India, the £1 sterling of the Indian currency will be the standard measure of the value of goods in exchange and the coin with which commercial balances between all but petty traders will be adjusted, as soon as the mercantile classes become accustomed to the new gold currency and appreciate the advantage of using it.

The arrangements proposed in this part of the plan are made with a view to provide the public with a legal method of discharging contracts to pay in rupees by the use of sovereigns, an initiatory measure which is absolutely necessary to introducing and setting up a circulation of the gold coin, but which will in the course of time become almost, if not entirely, obsolete by reason of a voluntary substitution on the part of the people of gold for silver coin as the basis of all important contracts. The greater the approximation may be to a general use of gold, the larger the demand for gold will grow, and the more profitable will it become for the owners of gold to coin their hoards into the currency and use them as money in trade. The merchant who is ready to pay in gold will always rule the market.

ARGUMENT FOR THIRD PROPOSAL.

Next comes the question of the rate at which the gold coins are to exchange for the silver rupees in the same currency. In the plan under discussion, the Government of India will fix a rate expressed in so many rupees for the sovereign, at which they will take the gold coins of their currency instead of silver rupees in payment of money to the State. At the same rate debtors will be at liberty to make payments due to be paid in rupees, if they please to do so. This rate will be fixed from time to time, as seldom or as frequently as may be convenient, in strict correspondence with the relative market value of the gold and the silver in either coin by public proclamation.

This plan of a "State rate of conversion" has been before the public now for three years, and while its correctness from the point of view of scientific theory has never been seriously disputed, the principal objection to its practical use is, that no Government will undertake the responsibility of saying how many sovereigns Rs. 5000 are worth. This really touches the personal idiosyncrasies of the officials on whom such a duty may be laid. That the Indian Government would shrink from such a task if supported by a sense of the advantage to be conferred on the people of that country directly and indirectly of the civilized world at large, and of the necessity of finding a way out of the financial troubles in which the declining and varying value of the silver currency involves the administration of the country, to which the use of gold as public money is a preliminary and absolutely essential step, can hardly be discussed as probable. What all the world knows, the Government of India can ascertain with the greatest certainty. The market value of the £1 sterling of the realm is quoted in every daily paper published in India, and it is merely futile to argue that the advisers of the Viceroy of India are likely to make a mistake, which no banker would make in his own business, in fixing a rate of exchange for the gold and silver coins of the currency in respect of payments into the public treasury. The Government would be the first to suffer if it were to make such a mistake, since if it materially undervalued the gold as against the silver coin of its currency it would receive none, and if it overvalued the gold coin it would lose on using those coins to make payments contracted to be paid in silver. This is a good guarantee for the exercise of care and caution. If more were required, the Government could get the best available information of the market value of its gold coin in the principal cities of foreign countries and in Indian markets almost from hour to hour by using the telegraph. It could watch from day to day the movement of the precious metals in the trade, and it would naturally consult, in the most public manner possible, commercial men whose opinion on such a subject might have a recognized authority as to the actual market value in India of its silver coin in terms of the gold currency, and by this means give confidence to the public that its interests in this matter were properly safe-guarded. The Government of India would have every inducement to fix a rate of conversion in exact correspondence with the ratio of intrinsic value obtaining between the two kinds of coin, and none whatever to do otherwise. Under these circumstances, no practical difficulties of an insuperable or even a serious kind exist against the use of a golden sovereign in the Indian currency along with the silver rupee on the terms above described.

It may be apprehended that the ratio between the two classes of coin would vary so frequently that the State rate for converting the silver into gold coin would be never constant.

The certainty of the value of money and the convenience of the public would be best secured by alterations in the rate of exchange being made no more frequently than might be necessary, and if it is apprehended that the frequency of such alterations would be in itself inconvenient, it will not be overlooked that they will not be more frequent, but less, under the system proposed, than the alterations which are daily made in the rates of exchange at which foreign bills are now sold. That fluctuations in the rate of exchange between gold and silver legal tender coins circulating together will have a tendency to diminish rather than to increase, must be the natural consequence of the two metals being used indifferently for the same purposes. If silver is in excess, and therefore falling in value against gold, while gold is stationary in quantity, silver will be exported and its value rise, and *vice versâ*. A decline in the value of either metal will be participated in by the other. The free use of both on terms of their intrinsic value will always operate, if not to narrow the ratio of value obtaining between them, at least to mitigate its fluctuations, and to render the point of equilibrium more constant. Under a system by which any amount of one metal will always exchange at its full natural value for a corresponding amount of the other, the capacity for mutual substitution, which makes gold and silver so suitable for money, obtains its highest development. It is only when they are divorced from one another by artificial currency regulations that gold and silver work in opposition. Allow them to work together in the order of their nature, and these divergences of value from which so much is feared must necessarily diminish, while the approximation to the attainment of a stable ratio of value will be correspondingly great.

The expectation is at least reasonable, that when gold and silver coins come into competition with one another and actually change hands at a valuation measured by the intrinsic worth of either, in numberless transactions great and small, and in widely separated localities, such a valuation will be ascertained with a much closer approximation to fact than is now the case where no such interchange is possible, and be established on a more reliable and permanent basis than that which it now rests on.

The gold quotations in the silver rupee of India are at present very much the result of transactions often more speculative than real in character, which are virtually arranged between a few individuals, instead of being, as they will be under the system proposed, the outcome of the daily traffic in commodities bought and sold with either metal indiscriminately in dealings to be counted by millions. The sale of the Council bills is in effect a sale of silver bullion for gold coin, because the price paid by the purchaser cannot be more than it would cost him to transport the same quantity of silver, for which he buys bills, as bullion to the East; but it is open to question whether this method is not inadequate for ascertaining the value of silver in India when exchanged for gold in the same country. The quotation of the value of the Indian sovereign in Indian rupees will, of course, under the plan proposed, approximate to the market rate of exchange at which bills payable in sterling in London are sold for rupees in India, but it may be safely predicted that it will rest on a basis exclusively Indian, regulated principally by the conditions of her own trade and the value of her gold coin in her local markets, and be therefore liable to much less fluctuation than a ratio of value established by methods which are quite independent of any competition between the two metals circulating together as coin in the country itself.

In point of fact, such fluctuations as can occur under the system proposed are of little or no importance to the public in general. A rise or fall in the value of the rupee by an eighth or a sixteenth of a penny has no effect on prices. The price of grain does not vary correspondingly. It is the business of the banker and of the speculator in the exchanges rather than that of the trader which is affected by them. From this class of financiers, opposition to any scheme for introducing the use of gold into India as coin is to be expected; because, as the stability of value between gold and silver coins as against each other increases, the opportunities of profit which they may now have by speculating in the exchanges will necessarily rather diminish than increase as the exchange becomes steadier. This is a matter of small moment to the public, and it must not be supposed that what is a cause of alarm to bankers and bullion dealers is therefore a matter of peril to the community.

RELATIVE VALUE OF GOLD AND SILVER ASCERTAINED BY THIS MEASURE.

Under these circumstances, the Indian currency will no doubt take the part which that of France for a long time played in the monetary world, as an equilibrating machine for establishing the true level of value between gold and silver. Whatever tendency to aberration local conditions in different countries may temporarily produce, the free competition of both metals as coin on the basis of their intrinsic value in India will offer at once an infallible standard for its detection and a means of correcting it. To India all men will turn to learn the daily value of the precious metals. India will justly claim to be the single country in which the commodities of the world are measured in gold and silver, and they in one another by a standard scientifically true and beyond the risk of deterioration from any external causes. Among secondary aids to commercial progress, the use of such a standard must take high rank.

As her commerce expands, increasing numbers of men and transactions of increasing value will fall under the influence of her commercial system. The use of a currency in which both metals circulate at their full value in one another will act as an inducement to traders to trade with India in preference to many other countries. Merchants will by preference contract to sell their goods in a market where they are paid in coin which is liable to no artificial diminution of purchasing efficiency. Investors will willingly lend money to a Government which pays in such coin, or provide capital for enterprises to which the returns are realized in so secure a form. So far as gold may become the standard of value in India, the country will reap all the benefits to be derived from payments due to her people being made in the more stable of the two metals. Her stock of gold will be continually replenished, and as gold will under such circumstances continue to raise the profits of all contracts which foreigners may enter into with the inhabitants of India, payments made under loans borrowed from them will acquire a gradually but constantly increasing value.

SILVER WILL BECOME MORE, NOT LESS STABLE IN VALUE.

It is not irrelevant here to refer to a criticism * of this plan for working a gold and silver currency together at a variable ratio of exchange between the two classes of coin, from the pen of a writer in the *Nineteenth Century.* Its scope and method he has misunderstood, and the conclusion he arrives at, that

* Extract from an article in No. 63 of the *Nineteenth Century.* "What is a standard?

"Mr. Clarmont Daniell, an Indian writer, proposes that there should be but one standard and one legal tender of money for all the world-gold. To this he adds, silver to be equally legal tender to any amount, but upon condition that its value as existing in the bullion market shall be ascertained from time to time and proclaimed by competent authority. Professor Bonamy Price supports this theory, and backs it by the singular argument 'that steadiness of value is incomparably the highest quality which money can possess.' He therefore wishes to take away that quality from that which is the money of a very large portion of the human race, simply because he is unwilling to accept one fact which Professor Jevons has proved to be mathematically correct, and another which the French mint prices show to be mathematically true.

"The objection which I feel both to Lord Grey's plan and to Mr. Daniell's is, that they have all the evils of a radical change without bringing us back to that state of the common measure of value which was lost when the French mint prices were given up. The use of a standard is, that if the unit be a pound, a dollar, a mark, a rupee, a franc, the persons having any number of these written against their names may know, as exactly as possible, what their debt is, and what quantity of what substance will suffice to free them from it. Now with a varying price between gold and silver, notwithstanding that both would be used as 'instruments of exchange between nations,' the above advantage would be lost."

to subordinate the rupee currency to a gold currency of sovereigns is to introduce instability into the silver currency of India, is open to question, both as a matter of theory and of fact.

Any one who carefully reads what has gone before, will not fail to perceive that the bulk of the internal commerce of India will, under the plan proposed, continue in the future as it has been in the past, unaffected by the gold price of silver, its stability or its variation. Goods will continue to be sold all over the country for silver rupees. A debtor with a rupee debt inscribed against his name will have to pay that debt in rupees, unless it exceeds Rs. 5000, and he elect to pay its equivalent in gold.

Except in the largest commercial cities and at the ports, gold and silver coin will not, for a long time, come into competition. Gold will not be used in the petty traffic of India's multitudinous bazaars. For all the influence that gold has on silver, the rupee in such places will buy just as much or just as little as it would have bought under any circumstances; and any rise of prices caused by the use of gold coin will be so gradual as to be imperceptible. It of course may be argued that a man who makes a payment of Rs. 12 with a sovereign one week, and a payment of Rs. 12¼ with another sovereign the next week, gains 4 anas by the latter transaction.

But this is a delusion. Under the plan proposed, such a payment could not be made except by the consent of both parties, for gold is not to be legal tender for a payment by one private person to another for sums under Rs. 5000. When such a payment is made by consent, the payee may be assumed to benefit by it, and no more need be said about it.

If the case is assumed of such a payment being made by law, that condition of things could only exist at some future time, when the use of the Indian sovereign had become so common in every bazaar as to be recognized as the measure of value for all commodities under all circumstances. It is obvious that when this happens, the goods under sale being measured by the sovereign used to pay for them, the same value of goods, if not the same quantity, would be sold in each week for that piece of money, and that the Rs. 12 the equivalent of the sovereign in one week, or the Rs. 12¼ its equivalent in the next, would be of the same value, because (as Euclid says) things which are equal to the same thing are equal to one another. The sovereign would in each week have bought a sovereign's worth of goods, and the varying amount of silver coin would likewise have purchased a sovereign, or a sovereign's worth of goods; and whether the purchaser were to use a sovereign, or a sovereign's equivalent in silver, he would in each week have got full value in goods for his money, although he may have paid a different quantity of silver money for the same quantity of goods in either week.

As long as the gold coin does not actually compete with the silver coin, the stability of value of the latter is unaffected; if the gold really but imperceptibly competes with the silver, the instability of the latter as a measure of value is expressed in a rise in price; if the gold visibly competes with the silver, it declares itself openly to be the true standard of value, and silver in that case entirely abdicates its function of a standard of value for goods under sale, and takes its own value from the gold coin. What really happens in the case upon which the essayist in the *Nineteenth Century* may be assumed to have argued is, that gold has replaced silver as a standard of value. If it is made a ground of complaint against gold that silver in this event loses its stability of value, the logical justification for such an objection is, that it is better for a nation to continue to use silver, a varying and declining standard of value in its commerce, because its defects are not startlingly obvious, and only work mischief gradually, than gold, which besides being exempt from such a defect, has this merit, that it invests all kinds of property with a more continuous and therefore a more certain value. Thus, to introduce gold into circulation in a market hitherto exclusively occupied with silver, and to exchange each kind of coin with the other on the basis of their intrinsic value, does not result in making the subsidiary silver coin less stable in value, but has the effect of making its inherent instability, both as against gold and as against commodities, more apparent than before, and at the same time, of substituting for it a less variable standard. This plan provides a method by which the owners of silver, when employing it in trade, will get their full value for their money, either in gold or commodities. This inducement, acting without restriction on the supply of either kind of metal, will call into use as coin the utmost quantity that commerce can require. The value of such a currency will be especially liable to gravitate towards the level of the cost of its production, and be proportionately less exposed to that kind of fluctuation which a sudden demand excites on a supply of money which cannot be easily or quickly increased.

The variations between the relative values of the silver money of India and the gold money of England, which now act as a serious restraint on trade, will, for these reasons, be neither so sudden, frequent, or excessive; and it may be safely predicted that the daily joint circulation of gold and silver coin at an unfixed ratio, so far from making silver less stable in the gold valuation than before, will mitigate the existing instability in their respective values. It will be no matter for surprise if it is discovered, when such a system has been fairly at work for a few years in India, that a tolerably permanent ratio of exchange between the gold and silver coins exchanging for commodities in the Indian market takes the place of that which so long prevailed. The commercial classes will cease to regret the disappearance of the 1 : 15½ ratio when its place has been taken by another, educed by the action of the natural laws of the cost of production and of supply and demand, acting on a free and unrestricted use of both kinds of money in the Indian currency.

Question of a Common Measure Examined.

In the same passage the writer objects that the plan under discussion involves all the evils of a radical change "without restoring the common measure of value" which the ratio of 1 of gold to 15½ of silver established. The justification of those who impose by law a fixed rate of exchange between coins current in any country is either that it is the natural and true rate of exchange, or, if it is an arbitrary rate, that it shall so work as to be fair to all men using it alike. M. Chevalier has told us that when the French currency was reorganized at the end of the last century, the ratio of 1 : 15½ was enforced because it was the intrinsic ratio prevailing between gold and silver, and the possibility that the legal would at some future time cease to correspond with the natural ratio was foreseen, in which case a recoinage of the gold currency was the expedient anticipated as a remedy for the divergence. The plan under discussion proposes that which is in principle the same remedy for a similar fluctuation of value, but without the ruinous expense attending a recoinage of an entire currency, which in the case of the Indian silver coin would require a mass of metal equivalent in value to no less than Rs. 420,000,000. The radical feature of the proposed change consists in the introduction into India of gold as legal tender coin, and in the establishment of a measure of value common to those countries with which the most important part of the trade of the country is carried on, and which shall at the same time be an equivalent as permanent in that character as it is in its function of a measure of value. When this change is effected, the Indian trader will know with a certainty, which he has been a stranger to for the last ten years, what value of coin will suffice for his business, since if he chooses to discharge with gold a contract payable in silver he will be no loser, because in a falling market his gold will command an increasing number of rupees; and if he has contracted to pay in gold, he will be able to dispense altogether with calculations of the silver value of the goods he is dealing in; and if he chooses to pay in silver, he can still do so.

The objection contained in the passage quoted above in fact involves the whole question, whether it is necessary for commerce that a fixation of value should be established between the gold and silver coins which in any country are current together.

A debtor under the system proposed knows quite as well as under any other currency system what sum of money is required to discharge his debt. If he, having undertaken to pay in silver, chooses to do so, he cannot be ignorant of the amount required to pay the debt. If he elect to pay in gold, its amount is easily ascertainable, and the creditor gets his full value for the silver due to him, and having regard to the tendency which under such a system gold has to rise, the gold payment he receives would not in the future be less efficient for trade or loan than the silver for which it was substituted. It is a mistake to speak of gold and silver when circulating together on the basis of their intrinsic values as constituting two different standards. Where either is used apart and beyond competition from the other, it is the single exclusive standard of the market. In those markets or those transactions in which the two metals come into competition, gold becomes the standard. This is a matter of fact which experience has placed beyond dispute. In a choice of standards all men prefer gold to silver. When gold is substituted for its equivalent value of silver, no loss can occur to a debtor paying a debt, nor undue gain to a creditor, nor can either feel uncertain about the value of the coin which will pass between them.

The system under which gold and silver circulated together in the French currency in unlimited quantities is spoken of by the writer in the *Nineteenth Century* as having provided a common measure of value, which has been lost since that nation ceased to maintain a fixed ratio of value between coins of the two metals. This common measure was lost because it was arbitrarily fixed by law, and as such laws are not obeyed when they are in conflict with the interests of the people, as soon as the condition of the bullion market, acting on the arbitrary fixation of the standard, created a field of profitable enterprise in the purchase of the over-valued with the cheaper metal, its uselessness as a common measure of value became immediately apparent. So long as the legal rate of exchange for the coins of the French currency corresponded, or nearly corresponded, with the natural ratio of value prevailing at the market between the two metals which they were made from, this common measure was maintained, but no longer. The common measure owed its efficiency to the fact that the coins exchanged on the basis of their intrinsic value and to nothing else. When from temporary causes the natural and legal ratio ceased to be identical, and the equilibrium got off its balance, it was restored by an increase in the supply of one metal or a diminution in that of the other. This went on as long as the balance oscillated over a curve of limited range, but to extend the metaphor, when silver became so light as to require not $15\frac{1}{2}$ but 18 times the weight of a given mass of gold to bring the latter metal up to its former level, a currency system designed to keep in equilibrium gold and silver in the proportions of $1 : 15\frac{1}{2}$ necessarily failed in its object. The plan now put forward, if properly worked, cannot fail to reconstitute this common measure in India, which has been lost in France. The essential principle is common to both that of exchanging the coins on the basis of their intrinsic value. In India, however, it will not be fixed by law at an immutable figure, but will from time to time be declared by competent authority *to be what it actually is at the time of the declaration.* Thus the natural ratio of value and the legal ratio must always coincide.

It is only with some qualification that the French currency system can be described as providing a common measure of value, if by measure is meant that which does not alter—a yard or a pound for instance. Under that system sometimes gold, sometimes silver, was the measure of value; when either metal became inefficient to measure the other, when, so to speak, a twenty-franc gold piece became too short to measure four silver five-franc pieces, or gold became overvalued, it disappeared and ceased to be a measure at all. What the French currency system effected was this: it gave the continental money-dealers a means of coining as much metal as they might wish, of testing by experiment the relative value of given quantities of either, and then of taking away the one of the two metals which they could employ more profitably outside France than within the limits of the country. The necessary result was that only that amount of either kind of coin remained in France which, under the influence of the ratio of value prevailing generally in the bullion market of Europe and America, could be circulated in the currency at the legal rate of exchange of 1 : 15½.

At such times as this condition was secured, and one kind of coin was not engaged in expelling the other from circulation, gold and silver can be correctly described as a "common measure of value," but at no other time. Circumstances latterly occurred which made it profitable to employ only one kind of metal, silver, at that rate, and highly unprofitable to employ gold at the same rate. Gold was, in consequence, disappearing altogether from France, and the Government of the country thenceforth gave up the attempt to circulate the two metals as coin together at a legal valuation which had ceased to be identical with the natural ratio of value existing between them as bullion. The French currency was a machine for distributing gold and silver over Europe, and even more distant parts of the world, in such proportions that the stock of gold remaining at home should nearly always be 15½ times as valuable as that of the silver. The French Government obtains the same result now by restricting very materially the coinage of silver, and by locking up a large portion of its existing silver currency, and so enhancing the value of the remainder; but this is done at the expense of the principle of the free coinage of both metals in unlimited quantities. If France were to adopt the natural ratio of value now obtaining between the two metals and coin, and exchange gold and silver in the ratio of 1 : 18 or thereabouts, its former system might (certain disturbing causes apart) flourish as it did before.

What the plan under discussion proposes for India is, that gold and silver should be a common measure of value for commodities ; but it differs from the French plan in that it secures this condition under all circumstances and under all fluctuations in the bullion value of the two kinds of coin. In France, on the other hand, this "common measure" was only found when the mass of the gold in the currency happened to be exactly 15½ times as valuable as that of the silver. At other times the two metals were not a common measure, but, approximately speaking, one or other became the single measure, and the discarded metal travelled abroad. In India, as in France, the owners of both metals will be free to coin them and use them as a legal tender money under regulations which will ensure that under all circumstances either exchanges for the other and both for commodities at their full market value. That which wrecked the French system, the fixation of the value of silver in gold, will be avoided in the system proposed for India. The mutual substitution of the two kinds of coin is, in the plan under discussion, provided for by the condition that the legal rate of exchange shall always be that which is dictated by the natural value of one of them in the other at the market. A conversion of one kind of money into the other cannot be effected on the basis of their relative intrinsic value under any other system yet proposed. That a state currency must be regulated by the Government of the country that uses it is evident, because it is the Government which must fix the amount of money of either description which it levies as taxes; and in order to secure certainty in the fulfilment of contracts, must declare what is and what is not a legal payment in discharge of debts. It is only on such terms that the owners of gold and silver coin will consent to exchange them for one another in commerce, when the coinage and circulation of both metals as legal tender money is free and unrestricted.

The length of time during which the ratio of 1 : 15½ actually obtained made it necessary throughout the Latin Union to coin silver and gold on those terms, and the difficulty and expense of reforming the coinage of the associated countries when the natural ratio began to differ from the legal ratio, in order to bring the currency value of their gold and silver coins into conformity with their intrinsic value in one another, were found to be enormous, probably insuperable. Of this any one can convince himself by a short arithmetical calculation of the cost of increasing the metal in the silver five-franc pieces held by France alone, by an amount sufficient to make four of them equal in value to one gold twenty-franc piece, and by a forecast of the effect that such an operation would have on the relative bullion value of silver and gold. The only feasible plan for using existing gold and silver coins in circulation together as legal tender money to any amount or value, is one of the characters proposed which provides for their exchange into one another without prejudice to either.

The author of this plan does not attempt, as has been erroneously stated, to advocate its adoption in Europe. However desirable or practicable such a course may be, it does not enter into the scope of this discussion to do more than show that in India no practical difficulties of an insuperable or even a serious character are opposed to the coinage and use as legal tender money of the stocks of gold existing in India under the system proposed.

When experience has proved how it will work in India, other nations will be able to judge how far such a system may suit the peculiar conditions of currency and trade which prevail among them.

The currencies of other countries besides England are becoming more rather than less monometallic with gold as a standard. In France a large portion of the silver coin is locked up, the remainder being used for the petty commerce of the country. Austria is said to be imitating the example of Germany, and to be getting rid of her silver. In America, the coinage of silver is limited; but indirectly uncurrent silver is used as a medium of exchange, by a system of certificates entitling the present holder to the possession of a store of silver held in reserve in the State treasury. The result of this state of things is considered to be an appreciation * in the value of gold as against commodities which operates to the disadvantage of those who have contracted to make fixed payments in gold during a term of years.

This appreciation in the value of gold can only be reduced in one way. If the internal trade of the United Kingdom requires 20,000,000 or 30,000,000 more of gold coin than it can now obtain, the want cannot be supplied otherwise than by using a corresponding quantity of silver in excess of that now current. This, however, is not possible where silver coin is token money, as it is in England; and as the silver coinage of foreign bimetallic countries is now managed, the supply of silver cannot be considerably increased without deranging the system into which the currencies of those countries have drifted. If it

* Speech delivered by the Right Hon. G. J. Goschen, in the House of Commons, on the 20th of February, 1883.

were possible to work a bimetallic currency with silver and gold coins, exchanging at an invariable rate without any limitation on the quantity of either in circulation, the appreciation, which is said to affect the value of gold in exchange for commodities, would of course disappear; since, if silver coin could be used in unrestricted quantities as legal tender money, it would supply the deficiency which is said to exist in the supply of gold coin. But if such a system cannot be established, and neither law nor convention suffices to give silver a value in gold which it does not naturally possess, then it is worth considering whether the plan of exchanging gold and silver coins on the basis of their intrinsic value will correct the artificial appreciation of gold or not.

Clearly, it must do so.

If (*e.g.*) throughout the Latin Union commodities are assumed to have fallen 20 per cent. in their gold valuation, in consequence of a restriction in the supply both of gold and silver coin, and if the quantity of the former cannot be increased, while that of the latter can be increased indefinitely, the use of a sufficient supply of silver to do 20 per cent. more work than is now done by the gold coin would necessarily bring prices to their former level. Without recommending this plan for general adoption, it is not irrelevant to show that an argument in support of its technical soundness as a currency system can be found in the existing condition of the coinages of some gold-using countries.

ALTERATIONS IN THE STATE RATE OF CONVERSION WOULD SELDOM OCCUR.

It will be remembered, that the receipt of a payment in gold for silver due, as between private persons, is only obligatory under this plan in a case where a large amount of money is involved, and only when the payer may elect to use gold On the other hand, the price of gold coin in the silver currency would be practically determined by an infinitely vast multitude of transactions throughout the country ; these would be settled, being of small amount, by the voluntary action of individuals at any rate of conversion which the parties in each case might agree upon.

Their transactions being below Rs. 5000 in value, they would, if they agreed to use gold, be at liberty to do so on any terms they might choose. It is by means of transactions of this kind that the real value of the gold and silver coins in one another will be evolved. It may vary somewhat in different localities in correspondence with some peculiarity of local demand for either kind of coin. But the practice of the chief cities, where such transactions will be numerous, will influence that of less important places, and the ease with which money can be carried about will tend to equalize the rate of exchange in conformity with that prevailing at the chief trade centres; and it will be to the rate prevailing in the latter places that those upon whom the duty falls of fixing the rate of conversion for the payment of taxes and large debts will principally look, in order to ascertain what the real relative value of the gold and silver coins in the currency is. The circumstances which regulate the sale of bills of exchange drawn on a foreign country payable in gold will not altogether govern the State rate for converting rupees into sovereigns in the Indian currency. In the former case, the demand for foreign bills, the credit of exporting firms who have bills to sell, the rate of interest prevailing abroad, the amount of money available for loans at home, all contribute to determine the gold price of rupee bills. But in the exchange of the two classes of coin in the currency, the demand for gold coin on the spot will principally regulate the price to be paid for it in silver.

The only true test of the value of Indian sovereigns in Indian rupees is the rate at which one passes in the other when both are used for the purchase of goods in the market. The value of English sovereigns (which are, in India, not money, but bullion), although it is daily quoted in the Indian newspapers at so many rupees apiece, is by no means an absolutely certain indication of what their value will be when their Indian counterpart is freely used as money along with the rupee. The Indian price of English sovereigns is largely influenced by the quotations of the value of silver bullion in the pound sterling in London, which depends on circumstances to a great extent independent of Indian considerations; and the rupee value of the sovereign is also affected by the course of trade, the demand or otherwise for those coins for exportation, and by the very important fact that the number of sovereigns in the Indian markets cannot be increased by the fabrication of fresh supplies of coin in the country, but that if more are wanted they must be obtained by importation from abroad.

As there can be no doubt that our present means for ascertaining the actual relative value of sovereigns and rupees when both are used together as money are defective, we may expect—when the coinage and circulation together of both is unrestricted, and their quantity only limited by the extent to which people may choose to use them—to see the values of gold and silver money take a somewhat different relation to one another from that in which they have been hitherto considered to stand, under the prohibition which the currency law of India places on the exchange of money coined out of either metal.

The State rate of conversion would always be under the pressure of a force constantly tending to ensure its accuracy; and if in any large market it were materially to vary from the market rate of conversion in vogue for small dealings, a withdrawal of the superabundant, or an importation of the scarcer metal, would immediately ensue, and the two rates of exchange would approach one another or become identical. The tendency of the market rate, when differing from the State rate, would always be to approach towards rather than to diverge from the latter, because capitalists and traders, having command of large stocks of coin, would be the class to use the State rate of conversion in settling their payments, and they would take care so to adjust the stock of either metal in the markets which they might be able to influence as to save themselves from loss in doing so. If a divergence of value originating in any permanent cause were to arise, Government would proclaim a fresh rate at which its coin would interchange, and this would become known in the course of a few hours at every considerable market in every quarter of the country.

It is not probable that the State rate of conversion evolved under these conditions, being the result of an actual competition between the two metals in use as coin, and following while it might appear to rule the rate of exchange, would require frequent rectification. The very frequency of the interchange of the coins is itself an element of stability of value. Government by accepting payments due to itself at its published rate of exchange would, from the magnitude and variety of the business it transacts, invest the State rate of conversion with an influence over all smaller and less important transactions, whether the use of gold in such payments were partially obligatory or quite optional. Government transactions and those of private persons would act and react on one another, with the result ordinarily obtained under such a process of uniformity and steadiness in the rate of exchange.

That the Government of India must be the ultimate referee and decide what shall be the rate at which its own coins are to exchange into one another, is an obvious and indispensable condition in the existence of a legal tender currency. To forbear from deciding on such a question would be to abdicate one of its principal functions as a Government; and as it would obtain the best information about the condition of the money market, and advice from many more sources than are available to private persons, the determination of the rate by a State official would necessarily command more confidence than could be secured for a rate of exchange ascertained by any private person, or in any other method than that already indicated.

That which has been done in other countries might, if the Government were to decline the duty of declaring the rate of exchange for the coins of its own currency, be done in India; and combinations among speculators in the exchanges be formed to depress or elevate artificially one or other kind of money in pursuit of their own profit.

The success of such schemes is possible where the State undertakes to pay, say, a fixed sum in gold for a fixed sum in silver or paper money; as, for example, when the United States undertook to redeem their paper currency in gold, an attempt was made to make a profit out of the necessity that Government was under to get gold, by a ring of speculators who contrived to prevent a sufficient supply of gold being immediately forthcoming. Under the plan of a State rate for the conversion of the coins into one another, such a scheme could never succeed. If gold were artificially restricted in supply, its silver price would rise, and those who would have before been inclined to purchase gold would leave it alone, and from being neglected it would immediately fall in value. Those already holding gold would in such a case benefit by discharging a silver debt in gold—but only in the event of the State rate of conversion having been altered in correspondence with the artificial enhancement, which in the case supposed had been contrived in favour of gold. But such an alteration is exactly that which Government would not under the circumstances make. If the rate for the conversion of the coins were liable to be fixed by any other association than the State, those who fix the rate and those who artificially enhance the value of the metal might possibly be the same persons. As the case stands, it would be apparent to Government that the enhancement in the value of gold was temporary and artificial, and not supported by the condition of the metal market, or by the state of the exchanges outside the local area, within which the speculators were operating—that is, throughout all India, and the principal cities on the continent, and in America. The speculators would be left with their accumulated gold on their hands. The public would use the gold currency on the authorized terms of exchange, or temporarily cease to use gold at all, and use silver instead; or gold would come into the market affected from many quarters, and its price in silver would fall. In any case, the combination would collapse in a dead loss to the speculators on the artificial rise.

Furthermore, the area over which such speculators would be obliged to operate, if they wished to engross any considerable portion of the gold coin of the country, would be too large for them to work in with any chance of success; for it would include all India, Australia, the China ports, and other more distant places.

If, on the other hand, their object were to enhance for their own profit the silver price of gold, in the hope that Government would buy it at their price, they would be easily defeated in this way. The Queen's dominions in India are divided into "districts," a few hundred in number. The "district" is the unit of the civil government of the country, and each district is the seat of a "treasury" of the Government of India, where taxes are received and disbursements on the public service are made. Any attempt which might be made in the large cities to enhance the price in silver of the gold currency, could, so far as it might affect the Government, be met by the latter inviting payment of its silver taxes in gold, at the market rate of exchange, at every one of these numerous local treasuries. Again, in order successfully to "corner" the Government on any occasion when it might seem likely to these speculators that gold would be required for State purposes, two conditions must exist: first, that Government should require a large quantity of gold coin, and next, that it should want it at once. But under a currency worked on this plan these two conditions never can arise. In no case will it be obligatory on any person or on Government to pay gold away; that is always optional. Silver being under all circumstances legal tender for any amount, the Government of India could never come (as far as a currency system worked on the plan under discussion is concerned) under the necessity of obtaining a large quantity of gold for State purposes, either within a long or short period of time.

If the case be assumed of the Government of India shipping the gold coin of India to London by way of "home" remittances, and speculators for a rise intercepted the supply, this form of remittance would at once cease, and the money required in London would be raised there by selling bills on India payable in gold or silver, or both, as might be convenient. A temporary and artificial restriction of the supply of gold coin circulating in Calcutta would not affect the price of these bills in London; and the causes which would fix that price would be necessarily too numerous and too remote from the influence of any ring of Indian speculators to be controlled in any degree by their operations.

Thus any apprehension that the "State rate of conversion" is, under any circumstances, likely to be regulated by manœuvres of this kind is seen to be groundless.

Loss by Exchange is more Apparent than Real.

The excess of commodities exported from India to England over those imported from the same quarter is paid for by imported treasure. Were the values of both imports and exports in equilibrium, there would be no balance left for settlement which had been unprovided for by the exchange of goods. The commercial balance is against England. But this is apparently not the case. The Government of India and the English in that country complain that the exchanges are against them when remitting money to England. If, however, the factors which contribute to this result could be dissociated, and the intrinsic value of the pound sterling in the Indian rupee, and the price of bills of exchange (as affected by other circumstances than the depreciation of silver in the gold valuation) be separately ascertained, the latter would probably be found to be favourable to persons remitting money from India to England. This advantage is, however, lost, and the contrary result attained, because the currency of India has fallen from its former value in the sterling money of the realm. So long as Englishmen in India cherish the delusion that Rs. 10 ought to be of the same value as £1 sterling, they will continue to talk about loss by exchange. Let the fact be recognized, that the par of exchange has altered from Rs. 10, to Rs. 12¼ or more for £1 sterling, and the exchanges will not then appear so unfavourable to India as they do now, or may turn out to be to the advantage of that country. The proof of this would be forthcoming if in India a legal tender gold currency identical with that of England were in use. If the par of exchange were thus restored, if sterling bills were sold in the Indian market for sterling money, then £1 sterling in the East would buy £1 sterling in the West; and if there proved to be a greater demand for bills on England in India than there is in England for bills on India, the latter country would get the benefit of the exchange, and £1 in India would buy £1$\frac{1}{40}$ or £1$\frac{1}{20}$ in England, and the present apparent loss by exchange would be converted into a visible gain.

The device of exchanging the gold and silver

coins of the Indian currency at a variable rate in correspondence with their relative intrinsic values would not affect the price of bills of exchange drawn by either country on the other, except indirectly and to a very slight degree, that is, to the extent to which the conversion at their true values of one kind of coin into the other would operate to prevent combinations arranged to create a fictitious rate of exchange. The influence of the State rate of conversion would invariably tend to steady the exchanges. The interference of the Government of the country would be confined to fixing the rate at which the taxpayer might convert his rupee payments into sterling, if he chose to use gold rather than silver money, and to fixing the same rate as that at which private persons paying debts of Rs. 5000 and upwards might do so likewise. The action of Government would in no way affect the price in rupees of sterling bills drawn on London. Any one buying such a bill for any amount, large or small, would make, as he does now, his bargain with the seller, equally whether he were to pay for the accommodation in silver or in gold. If, in such a case, the Government of India were to go into the market to buy bills as a means of remitting money to London, its own valuation of the gold coin in its currency would not impose any other price on such bills than that which they might naturally fetch. Indirectly, the fact that in India a local value for sovereigns is evolved out of their daily circulation as money with rupees will no doubt have an influence on the price at which sterling bills are quoted in the market. The purchaser of a £100 bill drawn on London will have a fair idea of what it is worth in rupees by the price which he has to pay for one hundred Indian sovereigns in that kind of money, but this is a result on every ground to be desired. It will tend to steady the rate of exchange by making the real value of the £1 sterling of the realm more easily ascertainable in Indian money, and avert much of that kind of loss which private persons now suffer from the use of two standards of value in the currencies of England and of India.

When a new par of exchange has been ascertained and established, the benefit of the exchange, so far as it depends on the relative indebtedness of either country, would probably be in favour of persons buying bills of exchange drawn by India on England; but in addition to the causes which ordinarily govern the price of such bills, there are others which are peculiar to the commercial and political connection existing between the two countries. The sea-borne trade between India and the West being carried by English shipowners, there must be a considerable debt due by India for freights. Many mercantile houses engaged in the Indian trade have their principal places of business in London, where commissions, profits, and similar transactions have to be settled. The returns to English capital invested in plantations, or machinery for the manufacture of textile fabrics, are to a great extent remitted to England. The English in India not being colonists, but merely residents, have occasion to remit week by week considerable sums of money to their own country for many necessary purposes; and, lastly, that part of the cost of administering the government of India, and of the interest on the public debt, and of the interest on the capital invested in guaranteed railways, which must be paid in London, amounts to £14,000,000 a year. These circumstances would operate to maintain the price of bills drawn on England, which might be offered for sale in India at a high figure; but whatever that might amount to, it would be the result of natural and automatic causes, and would be in no way attributable, as is now the case, to an exclusive and compulsory use of silver as coin in India.

The Secretary of State for India at present obtains the money he requires by a sale for sovereigns of rupees lying in the treasuries of the Government of India, the principal and material factor in the price paid being the value of silver bullion in the London market. When India obtains a gold currency, this operation will be no longer necessary; the Secretary of State will cease to figure as the largest vendor of silver in the world. The Government of India will then be able to purchase sterling bills on England with the sterling money in which part of the revenues of India will be paid, or will ship specie in the form of sovereigns to defray the home charges.

GOOD MONEY IS CONSISTENT WITH AN UNFIXED RATE OF EXCHANGE.

The principles above described, which control the exchange of money for commodities, operate with equal rigour in the case of coins made from different metals when exchanging with one another, provided that the supply of either kind is unrestricted in amount by any but automatic limitations, and that the rate of exchange corresponds with the relative intrinsic value of the coins in use. Let it be assumed that a given quantity of any article exchanges indifferently either for coins weighing one ounce of gold or for coins weighing sixteen ounces of silver, and as things which are equal to the same thing are equal to one another, the equation of value between gold and silver is at that time 1 : 16. If a sudden increase of gold, say of $\frac{1}{5}$, were made to the stock in use, the article under sale, which before exchanged for one ounce of gold money, would exchange for an ounce and a fraction, perhaps $1\frac{1}{10}$ oz.; but the same quantity of goods would still exchange for sixteen ounces of silver (putting aside for the moment any slight fall in the value of silver occasioned by an increased supply of current money), and the equation of value would then be $1\frac{1}{10}$: 16. If, during a long course of years, 1 : 16 were the ratio of value between gold and silver, that formula would describe the relative cost of their production ; and if the aberration from that ratio to another of $1\frac{1}{10}$: 16 were not occasioned by any permanent cause, but were owing to the temporary incidents of supply and demand, the respective values of the two kinds of coin would take again their original proportions. But whether this were to occur or not, it is evident that the gold and silver coins, when exchanging for one another, are ruled by the same laws which either kind of coin and commodities obey, and that the alteration indicates a real change of value, which if the equation had been artificially maintained at 1 : 16

would never have been expressed in the rate of exchange at all.

It has been objected that coins of which the value is not the same from day to day, that is to say, which do not always exchange for the same piece of gold, do not constitute true money. This, however, is a mistake. Any natural uniformity in the rate at which coins of one metal may pass in those of another is an accidental not an essential quality in money. In a few countries this uniformity is maintained in the interest of retail dealers by artificial contrivances, which induce peculiar evils of their own, and these have in their turn to be obviated or cured by remedies which complicate questions of currency otherwise very simple, and natural conditions are superseded by arbitrary laws and conventional expedients. That only can truly be called stability of value which is ascertained by the sale of one thing for another at a price fixed by the competition of traders. An uniformity in the ratio of exchange obtained by legal restrictions on the coinage of money, or on the amount of coins of one kind which may be given for those of another, is no guarantee of stability of value, and this becomes immediately apparent by the successful infraction of such laws, and by the disregard shown to the principles they embody, by those who are beyond their reach. A sham stability of value asserted in an artificial rate of exchange between two kinds of coin is at once challenged by the sale of commodities at different rates in the gold and in the silver coins of the currency, at prices which do not correspond with the conventional rate fixed for their interchange.

People in England have so long been accustomed to use gold and silver money in a fixed proportion of value, that the use of money on any other terms is deemed impracticable. In India, however, although for many years the East India Company's gold mohur was obtainable at Rs. 16, and the sovereigns of the English and Australian mints ordinarily passed for Rs. 10, yet the public are quite accustomed to the idea of silver and gold coins having a varying value from their daily experience of the fluctuations in the value of sovereigns and gold mohurs in the rupee currency. That gold and silver money circulating together as legal tender coin under conditions of a perfectly free exchange will pass at a varying rate of exchange in one another, is a circumstance of which the practical inconvenience will be subsequently shown to be insignificant, and, so far from exciting dislike to the use of both kinds of coin, will be regarded by the mercantile classes among the natives of India as a guarantee that their relative value is correctly ascertained, and expressed in the rate of exchange, since the State rate of conversion will be subject to the test of comparison with that evolved by the daily traffic of the bazaar.

Value is not like colour or weight, an inherent and substantial quality in money; it cannot be measured by a rule fixed by the processes of nature. The dynamic standard of a foot-pound maintained by the law of gravitation never varies, the linear yard is preserved at an invariable length by a metal standard; but the value of money depends on what it will exchange for, a condition liable to infinite variation, and legal ordinances for the valuation of current coin, are pernicious in the degree in which they interfere with complete freedom of exchange on the basis of the intrinsic value of the coins in one another.

If these arguments are sufficient to prove that the exchange value of money depends on the incidents of supply and demand, and ultimately on the cost of its production, it follows that any legal or arbitrary expedients which interfere with the free-working of these conditions must induce confusion into commercial business, while they cannot in the long run invest money with an efficiency exceeding its real value.

It is only in the case of a complete insulation of a currency, such as that which occurred in Japan previous to the seventeenth century, that the demand of those exchanging commodities for money fails to act on the real value of the coin measured by a standard common to all commercial nations. When the domestic currency of any country in which the nominal value is higher than the real value of the coin comes to be measured in the currency of a foreign country where the coinage and circulation of money is free, an arbitrary valuation of one kind of coin in the other fails in its operation.

That this is the case, may be illustrated by the analogy of coin of which the real value has become degraded below the standard or nominal value by wear and tear. Let it be supposed that the gold coin of the realm has on the average lost 3 per cent. of its mass by wear and tear, in this case a bill drawn from France, and paid for with a weight of gold coin equal to £97, would be reckoned at par if it procured £100 in England; but, nevertheless, if the price paid for the bill in France contain as much gold as were actually found in £98 English, then the exchange would be £1 in favour of England, although it would apparently be £2 to her disadvantage, judged by the standard or nominal value of sovereigns. Such a condition of the exchange was by no means uncommon at the end of the last century, when the currency of this country was in a very imperfect state, and foreign merchants settled their trade balances on the basis of the intrinsic and not of the nominal or standard value of the light-weight coin of England. The consequence was that the rates of exchange stated in terms of the standard coin confused and concealed the actual relation of value between English and foreign money.

Whether a distinction between the real and nominal value of current coin is occasioned by wear or by debasement of the currency, or by legislative regulations for the coinage and use of money, the same result follows ; in free commerce it is by the real not the nominal value of the currency that the prices of commodities within the country, and the rate of exchange for foreign bills drawn on the country, where these regulations prevail, will be adjusted.

This fact cannot be too clearly kept in view in every discussion on the comparative expediency of fixing by law, or by a convention of nations, the value of one kind of money in exchange with the other, or of allowing the two kinds of coin to pass at their intrinsic value in one another.

The practice which has prevailed in England since 1816, and within the last few years in France, of using silver coin in exchange at a nominal value, higher than its real value, in no way conflicts with this argument, because in both countries the silver currency is practically insulated, and effectual precautions are taken against its quantity being increased by an amount which would deprive the coin of its artificial value when exchanging with gold. The silver coin of those countries never comes into competition with the silver coin in unrestricted circulation in foreign countries, because both the English and French settle international trade-balances in gold, although in the case of the latter the gold used is described in terms of its conventional valuation in silver. As goods in the French trade are described as being sold for francs, it always appears that they are sold for silver, and similarly bills of exchange drawn on France in terms of francs appear to be sold for their real value in the latter coin; whereas in either case the sale price is actually regulated by a valuation calculated in the gold currency of England and France respectively. Were France to adopt the rate of exchange of 15½ ozs. of silver coin for 1 oz. of gold coin, and to allow a perfectly free coinage to gold and silver in her mint, bills purchased for rupees in India, if they were payable in silver in France, would draw an equal value of silver in francs, calculated at their intrinsic value, without reference to the ratio of 15½ : 1; and if such bills were payable in gold in France, their price in rupees in India would be fixed by the intrinsic value of silver in gold metal, without reference to the fact that the silver coin of France was rated at 15½ : 1 in the gold coin of the same country. Thus the arbitrary fixation of one kind of coin in the valuation of the other can only induce confusion into trade transactions, and under a system of free coinage can have no effect on the value of the coin in exchange for commodities, or in any way influence the value set on the domestic currency of the people who exchange their gold and silver coin at an arbitrary valuation by foreign nations in their dealings with them.

CASE FOR AN ALTERATION OF THE RATE OF EXCHANGE.

It may be objected that a producer buying his material and paying for labour with rupees might find the ratio of value to have altered between the date his goods were brought to market and the date of their sale. Let us assume that he fixes his price at Rs. 5454 8a. 8p., calculated to give him the ordinary profit of his business on the transaction. This sum of rupees at 1s. 10d. per rupee he might be required to take payment for in £500. If before he could convert his sovereigns into silver the rate of exchange rose to 1s. 10$\frac{1}{16}$d., the vendor would only get Rs. 5439 1a. 8p. in the market, which would be the silver price of his manufacture. On applying this money in his business, he would find that the cost of commodities and labour had not altered in correspondence with this rise in the value of silver against gold, and he would be unable immediately to recover this loss of Rs. 15 7a. 3p. on £500. Prices, if tending towards an alteration, would be inclined to fall rather than rise; but the rise of one-sixteenth in the value of silver as against gold would not necessarily result in a fall in the silver prices of commodities brought for sale in silver. If the trader were dealing in produce raised in a part of the country where the influence of gold had not yet reached, the vendor would have a smaller sum of money then he counted on wherewith to commence a fresh transaction, and would be a loser by being paid in gold instead of silver. This illustration describes that which daily occurs in the foreign trade of the country (except that silver generally falls rather than rises as against gold), and, under existing circumstances, the loser and an innumerable succession of losers after him are left to bear their losses or risks of losses, while no attempt is made, or is even contemplated, to diminish those risks by an improvement in the Indian currency. If an appreciation of silver against gold were to occur, and its importance and the probability that it arose from permanent causes justified an alteration in the State rate of conversion, the necessary revision would under the system be made, and future risk of this kind of loss would be eliminated from the traders' calculations.

If, however, the dealer in produce were tolerably skilful, he would anticipate the decline in the value of silver, and provide against this risk by asking a slightly enhanced silver price, and so obtain a payment in gold which, converted into silver, would yield him the desired sum of profit in that coin. On the other hand, although on exchanging his £500 into silver, the trader may get less silver than he previously counted on, the diminished quantity of silver will, in the market where he sells his goods for gold, avail to purchase more gold than was possible before, and in any business for which he may purchase gold with silver he will gain to the same extent that he had lost in the case assumed; and if he trades with silver in that market, all commodities offered for sale therein being regulated by the gold standard, the amount of silver into which he may have converted the gold will be as efficient for purchase as the gold itself. In the first case, the effect is seen of a rise in the value of silver in an area of production or manufacture where silver exclusively regulates values and gold does not compete with the baser metal at all. The silver prices of commodities remain practically unaffected (or at least are but very slowly affected) by variations in the value of silver when measured in gold in the bullion market, or in distant centres of trade.

But, in the second case, if gold and silver are both circulating together as legal tender coin, the liquidation of a contract for payment in silver by a payment in gold cannot result in loss to the payee, since the gold used for payment is equal in value to the silver, and all the commodities in that market, silver among them, are priced by the gold standard. It may also be safely predicted that transactions in a locality where the prevailing use of gold has caused it to become the standard of value will be carried through with gold, and in a very short time the case of a silver payment being made at the option of the payer in gold will become very rare. It is necessary, however, during the period of transition from the use of silver to the use of gold, to provide a means by which gold payments can be made the legal liquidation of silver debts.

In producing goods for sale in a market where gold prices prevail, the manufacturer would, in bringing his goods to sale for gold, reckon his expenditure of silver in manufacturing them, as he reckons every other item of the cost of production. The silver coin (or for that matter the copper coin) he may spend in paying labour or buying raw material would be regulated in its amount by the gold price which he might reasonably expect to get in lieu of the silver price, at which he would calculate the value to him of the article he was manufacturing. This being the case, and payment for goods being made with gold, if the silver returned to the vendor on the conversion of the gold price into that coin is less than he expected, then the trader is proved to have overvalued his goods at their silver price in the market, the value of the quantity of goods he offered for sale would turn out to be less than Rs. 5454 8a. 8p., the supply of the article as contrasted with the demand for it being considered.

The silver spent by the manufacturer, and every other expense incurred in bringing the commodity to sale, fixes the minimum price at which he can profitably sell it; the gold price is determined by the lowest rate at which the commodity can be sold for gold throughout the whole market, without reference to the particular expense which each separate producer is put to for his share of the bulk of that article offered for sale at the time. If the vendor loses on the transaction, he is unfortunate or unskilful. His loss may not be his own fault, but it is not the fault of the gold or the silver coin current in the market, nor does it arise from their interchange on the basis of their intrinsic value.

It is too obvious to require argument for its proof, that in a market or in an area of production in which gold regulates values, and in which silver is used indifferently with gold as money, the cost of production and the ultimate price being regulated by the same standard, no serious variation of real value arising from the use of both metals as currency can occur between that of the labour and materials used for the manufacture of any commodity at one time, and similar labour and materials used on producing fresh supplies of the same article at a little later date. The money which the manufacturer gets for his goods, be it gold or silver, will be equally efficient for the latter as for the previous operation. When this is not the case, the declining efficiency of money for purchase arises from a general rise of prices, and is not attributable to any such cause as a variation in the value of the silver and gold coins in the currency when exchanged for one another.

ARGUMENT FOR FOURTH AND FIFTH PROPOSALS.

The fourth of the foregoing proposals is, that the silver rupee of India shall, under all circumstances, continue to be legal tender for the payment of any kind of debt. Thus, while in some cases a debtor may compel his creditor to take gold, no creditor can compel a debtor to pay gold. The use of gold is, for large transactions, optional on the part of the *payer*. The use of silver is, under all circumstances, lawful. The Government of India, it is proposed, should agree to take gold at the State rate of conversion in payment of any debts due to itself however small, but will be in no way bound to pay gold away. When Government chooses to do so, in making payments of Rs. 5000 and upwards in value, it will be able, like private individuals, to compel the recipient to take gold at the authorized rate of conversion. The efficiency of silver as legal tender money will remain unimpaired, and its coinage, as it is now, be unrestricted in quantity.

Silver will also be sometimes used in completing gold payments in such cases as the following. If a debtor were to pay a debt of Rs. 5000 in gold, and the rate of conversion were Rs. 12 for a sovereign, he would pay £416, the equivalent of Rs. 4992, and

Rs. 8 of the silver currency, because there would be no gold coin current equal to Rs. 8. If the Government were to issue half-sovereigns, then, of course, in the case assumed, £416½ would be paid in gold and Rs. 2 in silver. Such a use of both kinds of coin in combination would be obviously extremely easy and cause trouble to no one.

The fifth proposal is only inserted to make it more clear that the silver currency of India remains unaffected as legal tender money.

EFFECT OF DISPLACED SILVER ON THE PRICE OF GOLD.

The apprehension at first sight seems not altogether groundless, that to change a portion of the Indian currency from silver to gold coin will still further lower the value of silver, which would fall against gold in correspondence with the quantities discarded; that the conversion of rupees into sovereigns could only be effected by a continually increasing quantity of silver; and that the financial difficulties of the Government instead of diminishing would increase.

But those who argue thus have overlooked certain results arising from the introduction of gold coin into the currency of India, which in the ordinary operation of cause and effect would prevent silver falling in value against gold in the manner such an objection anticipates.

One effect of the use of gold as coin would be to stimulate production in India by the wider market which it would open to the sale of her commodities. This increased production can only be effected by an increased expenditure of silver coin, that is, by an enlargement of the annual increment now made to the Indian currency of £8,000,000 or £10,000,000 worth of silver; and the silver, or a large portion of it, on being displaced from use by gold would be absorbed in increasing the natural productions of the country. Silver coins must necessarily, from the low price of labour and the necessaries of life in India, continue for many generations to be the popular money of the country.

Another effect of bringing the hoarded gold into use as coin would be to increase the world's stock of coined gold in the form best calculated to extend its use in commerce. Sovereigns would necessarily become cheaper in the silver valuation with every million issued from the mints, until this tendency were checked by the demand for the gold coin increasing in correspondence with its declining value. This, of course, might occur very soon, and even before any material alteration of value had taken place. If silver were discarded in favour of gold, the mass of silver bullion would, from increasing redundancy, fall in value against gold coin; but this would be quite a different thing from silver coin falling in value against gold coin. Silver, on the other hand, as fast as any of the discarded stock were brought again into use for the purchase of fresh supplies of gold for coinage, would, under the influence of the law of the proportion between the amount of goods under exchange and the amount of money used in exchanging them, experience an increase of exchange value on that it held when discarded. The additional employment given to silver under the stimulus which an extended use of gold is assumed as giving to the productive energies of the people, would also act towards a rise in exchange value. These and other causes would go far to prevent a fall (if they did not completely succeed in averting it), and in any case would prevent violent oscillations in the rate of exchange for gold money in use.

It is with the latter condition that the financial authorities of India would have to deal. The gold and silver with which they would be concerned in future would in all cases be money. Nor, as is now the case, would first one metal and then the other be for the purposes of their business bullion.

The value of gold and silver money in free circulation together does not depend in their interchange on the proportion between the quantity of either in use and the quantity of bullion of the same metal out of use. It does not follow that when silver may be discarded to some extent that the value of the silver coin will fall in a corresponding degree against the gold coin of the same currency. The efficiency of both kinds of money for the purchase of commodities depends on their quantity as contrasted with the work they have to do, and the same cause will regulate the efficiency of either for the purchase of the other. If Rs. 50 or £4 will indifferently purchase a given quantity of goods, either sum will purchase the other. The apprehension that the use of gold will lead to the discarding of silver, and thence to a fall in the purchasing power of silver money, arises from the existing condition of the currency of India. People see that when the price of silver falls the price of rupees in sovereigns falls also, and this is because the Indian rupee currency is liable to be increased if a higher than the bullion price is given for rupees. In the event, however, of gold becoming legal tender coin and the standard of value in the currency and commerce of India, the gold coin of England will purchase the gold coin of India, and the price of bills of exchange will tend to seek the specie point, not of silver, but of gold. Silver coin in use in India will necessarily take its value rather from the demand for it for use as money in that country than (as is now the case) from the bullion value of silver in sovereigns. That the cheapness of silver bullion will have some effect on the quantity of that metal coined from time to time into the currency is not to be denied, but that effect has been much overrated. Facts very clearly prove that additions are not made to the Indian rupee currency in correspondence with a decline in the value of silver bullion.

This is evident from some facts brought together in a recent discussion on this subject by a contributor to the *Westminster Review.** He remarks that "At those times when silver has been dearest, the largest additions have been made to the currency of India; and in more recent years, when silver has been cheap at the gold valuation, the yearly increment has been least. Thus, in 1856, and 1857, and 1859, when the price of silver ranged from 60¼d. to 62¾d., and between 1863 and 1866, when the average price continued slightly above 61d., more than seventy

* *Westminster Review*, No. cxiii. p. 135.

and a quarter millions sterling were added to the silver currency of India, at an average rate of more than ten millions per annum; while, on the other hand, in the period between 1873 and 1876, when the price of silver ranged from 50d. to 59¼d., the average yearly increment was considerably less than five millions."

Additions are only made to the currency as commodities in increasing quantities come into the market to be exchanged for one another, and it therefore will be in the case assumed a matter of secondary importance whether silver bullion falls or does not fall when priced in the gold money of India. It will be on the exchange value of one kind of coin with the other that the attention of the Government will be fixed, and this will be principally regulated by the increasing or decreasing quantities of commodities under exchange for one another, that is, by the requirements of the whole commerce of the country, and only in lower degree by the price of silver bullion.

Finally, if the contrary were the case, and silver money were liable to fall in value against gold money as silver bullion became cheaper, it would follow that as fast as this occurred fresh silver coin would be added to the Indian currency; since, on this assumption, it is only by being coined in increased quantities that the cheapness of bullion causes a decline in the exchange value of money. But additions to the rupee currency are not made from such a cause now, and they therefore in future will certainly not be made from the same cause when gold coin is in use exchanging for silver coin at its intrinsic value.

The example of the French currency, which at first sight appears to contradict this theory, really proves it. The French gold currency was in danger of being bought up with coin of the silver currency, which it was reasonably expected would be fabricated in large quantities with this particular object, irrespective of the demands of French commerce for silver coin, and the reason of this was, that the French law for the interchange of gold and silver coins rated the gold coins at 20 per cent. below their value in silver. If the rate had been fixed on the basis of the relative intrinsic value of the two kinds of money in circulation, one could not have been used to buy up the other; for the purchaser would gain no profit in doing so, and speculators would have at once perceived the futility of adding more silver coin to the currency in order to buy up the gold coin, when by doing so they would have to give proportionately more of the former for the latter than they gave before.

N

It therefore follows that the value of the silver coins of the Indian currency, when exchanging with the gold coins, will not depend on the bullion value of silver in gold, but on the demand which commerce may make for silver in preference to gold for use as money. This demand, however, cannot, under the regulating influence of the exchange on the basis of their intrinsic values, occasion either sudden or great variations in the relative value of the two kinds of money, because any material additions made to one kind will cause it to fall in value against the other to the same extent to which (from that kind of money being redundant) its value would fall against commodities.

The argument cannot be too plainly urged which has run through some part of this discussion, that necessity and expediency, to say nothing of the duty of the ruler to his people, combine in favour of an unrestricted use of either kind of metal as coin at their actual value as the true and only remedy for embarrassments, which have their origin in the employment of the inferior metal and in the exclusion of gold money from use in India. Until unlimited space for free play is accorded to the action of the two natural forces of the cost of production and of supply and demand in the currency as well as in the commerce of India, nothing but loss and confusion continually recurring in new forms and fresh combinations will be the result. The evolution of a new and true ratio of value for silver and gold money in the Indian currency by the action of natural causes is the great desideratum. The surest means to secure that end should be taken, and the issue may then be awaited with an assurance that whatever it may be, it will be that which best serves the commercial interests of the people of the country.

The objection that an increased use of gold coin involves a decline in the value of silver coin would have weight if there remained no field open for the use of the discarded silver. Such, however, is by no means the case.

The stocks of gold now held in India are there for some purpose. The Indian people have not accumulated £112,000,000 sterling in gold in forty-seven years for no reason at all. Gold coins and gold blocks serve as a medium for making remittances, and are hoarded as a security against the vicissitudes of fortune, or as a resource to fall back upon in times of political convulsion. Gold is largely held by bankers, whose acknowledged possession of a stock of gold is the foundation of their commercial credit. As a hoard to be laid up against bad times, silver is nearly as useful as gold, and if the owners of gold saw their profit in using it in trade, a large part of their gold treasure would doubtless be replaced by silver. Bankers and other traders who now possess gold would, for a similar reason, substitute for it silver.

This practice of hoarding coin is by no means without advantage to commerce. When currency tends to become redundant, prices rise, and fresh accretions to the stock of coin fall off. The surplus money goes away from the country, or is hoarded, as it is in India; hoarding, therefore, is beneficial in its tendency to rectify a too-frequent variability of ratio between gold and silver, by reducing the quantity of the more abundant metal.

The extension of the market for the productions of India by the use of gold money in the currency is not the only stimulus it affords to her industry. If it were the case that silver, from being discarded, declined in value as against commodities in India, the rise of prices which would result would have an immediate effect in increasing production, and thus would create a demand for further supplies of silver coin, and, so far as this might be the case, the fall in the value of silver against gold would be proportionately arrested.

The continuous demand for silver from Asia, no doubt, keeps up its price at the tolerably steady figure about which it has ranged for some time past;

and if the metal which India annually absorbs—to the value on an average of £8,000,000 or £10,000,000—were gradually reduced, existing inducements to the mining of silver would be correspondingly removed, less fresh silver would be excavated, and a fall in its value by this means mitigated.

All these causes would be in operation at once, and have no other tendency than to prevent a fall—and much more a sudden fall—in the value of silver as measured in gold. The establishment of a gold currency in India will be a work of time and very gradual in its process, and the best security that the country can have that the existing condition of the metal market will not be violently disturbed, is found in the provision that the coinage of gold under the plan proposed should be limited by the amount of bullion which the people of the country may themselves bring to the mints. As the proportion in which gold may be introduced into and silver displaced from the currency will depend on the volition of the people themselves, no fear need arise that they will do injury to their own interests by too great a haste in discarding their silver from use. Bullion dealers, no doubt, hearing that the Indian Government is about to coin gold, would calculate on the discarding of silver, and would endeavour to sell their stocks while they could. The exchange banks would, for a similar reason, make the use of gold as money in India a pretext for raising the silver price of gold bills. The best way of preventing the occurrence of these eventualities would be for the Government to make as public as possible, some time before it was introduced, the scheme they might adopt for using gold money in India. Speculators would then wait and see how much gold was brought to the mints for coinage into money, and how much silver was discarded, and what rate of exchange between the two metals would be the outcome of the actual circulation and use indifferently of both kinds of coin in the Indian markets on the basis of their intrinsic value.

Stability of Silver Values in India.

The question has been asked why it is that although silver has fallen during the last ten years some 20 per cent. in the gold valuation, prices calculated in the silver currency of India have not risen correspondingly. The theory that the exchange value of money (and in this particular case silver money is in question) is regulated by the proportion between the goods in commerce and the money in circulation accounts for this circumstance. Although the silver coin of that country has in recent years been largely increased, the quantity of goods in commerce has been increased also. Prices at the principal centres of trade are probably higher than they were ten years ago, as in such places the influence of the new coin on the money value of commodities would be more active than in remoter situations, and money and goods would have taken a slightly different proportion to one another than they held before. Merchandise, the subject of export abroad, will be found to have been affected in a more decided manner, because when goods are taken from a cheap to a dear market, their value shows a tendency to rise in the former to the level obtaining in the latter. They are confronted in both *markets together* with a larger amount of money than was in circulation in the market of production. The jute tea or indigo of India are exchanged for other commodities, not only by means of the rupees circulating in that country, but by means also of the sovereigns and eagles circulating in England, Australia, or America. So far as the people of those or other foreign countries buy goods in India, they bring those goods within the scope of their own currencies. The Indians, although they may not be able to trace the effect to its cause, find that as their exportable production are being exchanged both among their own people with their own money and among foreigners with foreign money, they obtain the advantage of a demand made by a larger number of customers using a proportionately larger amount of current money for the purchase of the whole stock of articles of this description which are offered for sale in India.

Whether silver has become cheaper by a diminution in the cost of its production, or by a redundancy in the stock in consequence of the metal being discarded as coin, silver money will not be less efficient for purchase than before, so long as the increased amount of money which has been coined into the circulation is not more than is required to exchange the increased commodities brought into the Indian markets. Although silver bullion may have fallen 20 per cent. in value when measured in gold, so long as the stock of silver money which is exclusively used as currency in India only increases in the same proportion that commodities in commerce increase, prices will, on the average, remain unaltered.

THE CUSTOM OF BARTER SHOULD BE DISCOURAGED.

In a country like India, whose commercial arrangements in some places approach those of the more civilized nations of Europe, and in other places are not much advanced beyond those of very primitive communities, it is of primary importance to familiarize the more backward populations with the superior advantage attending the use of money over purchases by barter and book credits, and the payment of labour in coin rather than in grain or provisions. It is only by putting it within the power of the ryot to insist on receiving money wages for his labour, and to pay ready money for his food and clothing, that the Government will effectually succeed in protecting him against famine by giving him the means of saving money or storing his crop, and thus improving his condition. At the same time, a continuous development in the public revenues, whether derived from land-rent or taxation, would be secured with the increasing prosperity of the producing class. In order to this end, the stock of coined money now in British India must be much increased.

The extent to which barter is resorted to in the daily life of the Indian labourer and artisan, and the numbers of people who live on food borrowed from day to day, on the credit of the next harvest, and the amount of wages which is paid in provisions, can be with difficulty understood by those accustomed to European methods of business. The Indian magistrate or revenue collector, having daily experience of these customs, soon ceases to notice them as unusual. The influence, however, which they exert as restraints on industry is, from an economical point of view, of enormous importance; and any measure tending to improve a condition of the labour market so injurious to the people at large, claims attention on this, if on no other ground.

At present, the quantity of silver in use in India is by tale less than ten rupees per head of the population, while throughout all Europe it is estimated at the equivalent of about Rs. 21 per head. No account is taken of copper or of paper money in either case. The Indian populations may, therefore, be said to be grievously in want of money. This they can only supply themselves with by increasing their productions under the stimulus of high prices, and one step in that direction is to liberate silver and extend its use by employing gold in the currency of the country.

The Government of India has shown much wisdom in disregarding all persuasion to extricate itself from the financial difficulty known as "loss by exchange," by enhancing in any artificial manner the exchange value of its silver currency. Recommendations of more than one kind have been urged on its notice to diminish the quantity of coin in circulation, and thus increase its purchasing power. To these the Government has fortunately turned a deaf ear, and so averted a serious calamity which at one time seemed impending over the people. The higher price which people with incomes in silver have to pay for sovereigns now than they paid ten years ago, has so far dominated men's ideas on this question that they fail to perceive its economic and social aspect, and look at it solely from the point of view of bills of exchange.

To limit the quantity of coin in circulation in India, to omit any effort to provide facilities for the free coinage and use of all kinds of money, would be, in the present condition of her people, the greatest financial blunder which the rulers of that country could commit. Although much has been done, much remains to be done, especially in the field of financial administration, to improve the condition of the masses; and one obvious requirement is to give them the means of supplying themselves with as much coin as they require. An enormous proportion of the lower class of people are not only habitually in debt, but are insufficiently fed and clothed, and are always on the verge of starvation. A very slight increase in the cost of provisions brings peasant families in great numbers down to one meal in two days, and to the use of weeds and berries as food. This prevalent poverty will only disappear with an abundance of money. When this is acquired, the ryot will sell his crop for cash, and buy food of the kind and at the time he may want it, instead of "trucking" at the provision shop, where he has to take what he can get at a price fixed by the vendor, on which interest is charged until the account is settled. When money becomes plentiful, he will get the best price in the market for his wheat or millet, and spend the money as he may find convenient.

Now he bargains with a neighbour over the exchange of a bag of corn for a little salt, a petticoat for his wife, or a pair of shoes for himself. Yet it is this barbarous condition of trade that those who recommend a restriction on the quantity of money in use would, perhaps without knowing it, perpetuate and intensify. If the people were allowed an unlimited right of coinage, and a free circulation of gold and silver money were set up, the currency would be replenished to the full. Experience teaches us that under such conditions coin will be added to the circulation in quantities progressing in the ratio of the volume of commodities, and of the ease and celerity with which they exchange together. Facilities for trade are yearly expanding, and the demand for fresh coin more than keeps pace with extensions of commerce. An abundance of money in circulation results in a high price of produce and a low rate of interest. Its diffusion is more general, the number of money-lenders increases, and that part of the population which, as they are now situated, must borrow to live at all, will have a choice of creditors and obtain their means of subsistence on easier terms.

The importance of this kind of alleviation in the hard life of the working classes in India will be recognized by all who are acquainted with their condition, or whose business has given them experience of the petty tyrannies and extortion of the village grain-dealer and money-lender.

The ascendency of this class in their character of creditors, among the cultivating proprietors and tenantry, gives them a comparative monopoly in the purchase of produce, and the price at which they choose to buy is in practice that which the seller must accept. The emancipation of the agricultural classes from this kind of serfdom can be effected by no means which omit to provide for the unrestricted coinage of as large a portion of the gold and silver bullion now in India, and the free circulation of both kinds of money, as the people may by their own action bring into use.

Prices do not answer quickly to a fall of one precious metal in the valuation of the other. During the ten years in which silver has fallen about 20 per cent., some commodities have been scarcely affected in price, and none have risen very much. The reason of this is, that the Indian silver currency is supplied by the action of the people themselves in just such quantities as they require it. With the assistance of credits, paper contrivances for circulating money, barter and payment in kind, it suffices for their wants in the present condition of the country. The amount of the currency corresponds with the amount of work it has to do in exchanging commodities, and it is increased as the commodities brought into the markets increase. If those commodities, or that part of them which exchange for coined rupees, were suddenly to increase 20 per cent., then India would simultaneously require an addition of 20 per cent. on her present stock of coined money. If coin in the proportion of 20 per cent. were added at a stroke to the Indian currency, then prices would rise accordingly. But no such violent alteration in the amount of goods or of coin in the market has taken place. This is the reason why silver, although its value when competing with gold has fallen about

20 per cent. since 1870, has not lost its efficiency for the purchase in India of produce in any such proportion.

The coined money of the currency has not been increased by 20 per cent., or by any sum at all approaching 20 per cent., on the figure at which it stood in the beginning of this decade; and such increase as has been made to the stock of currency during that time has been almost entirely absorbed in the production of increasing quantities of raw and manufactured goods, in supplying outlying districts hitherto in want of coin, or in constructing communications, and so equalizing the values of produce in distant places.

Silver prices in their general steadiness have only expressed the fact that, although coined money and productions have both increased in the last ten years, the proportion previously existing between them has been closely maintained.

It must not be forgotten that although gold has, in the last ten years, risen some 20 per cent. on its former value in silver, and other commodities have not done so, there is no proof in this condition of things of the existence of two values in the same market for the same article. Gold in India is bullion. If gold legal tender money had been circulating in India during the last ten years, prices would have adjusted themselves to the rise in the value of gold; but no gold money having been in use, prices have adjusted themselves to the only measure of value existing in the country, and gold bullion, like any other commodity, has taken its present value (of about Rs. 20 instead of Rs. 16 per tolah) from that standard.

Reason why a Sudden Rise of Prices will not occur.

As goods come to be customarily sold for gold in the Indian markets, the demand for them may be expected to rise, in consequence of the convenience to trade which the use of gold as the money common to the Indian producer and the English consumer will secure. The increased demand will be followed by a rise in the price of exportable articles in India, and by a gradually and imperceptibly diminished purchasing power in the silver currency.

As the goods whose price would thus rise are only a small portion of all the goods in exchange, the effect of a rise of their value on the purchasing power of all the money in India will correspond to the proportion in which they may stand to all the goods under exchange for money, and will necessarily be but slight. At the same time, the quantity of money will itself increase in consequence of this rise in prices. The supply of silver, from which the call for fresh money can be answered, is out of all proportion larger than the demand for it, and bullion will continue to be coined into money as fast as any profit, however small, can be obtained by doing so. Under these circumstances, the fall in the value of silver money in consequence of any expansion which commerce may experience from the use of gold money will either be very slight or amount to nothing at all.

All accessions to the treasure or coined money of any nation are first appropriated by a few individuals, or a limited class of people. They soon distribute their surplus wealth among producers, whose livelihood depends on the vigilance with which they watch the requirements of consumers. Prices never rise universally and suddenly. First one commodity is affected, then another, some more and some less; others cease to be in demand at all, being superseded by other more useful articles. The value of commodities, like the height of trees in a forest, is of gradual growth. Although all the trees may grow together, they never grow at the same pace; some grow quickly, some slowly, some are overshadowed by others and die down. Some goods under the stimulus of a high price are produced in greater quantity than before, and, perhaps, ultimately fall in value relatively to other commodities, whose rise in value has been more gradual and permanent. A proportion will always be maintained between the values of different articles, although it may be very different from that existing in a previous generation; and men adjust their expenditure, their mode of life and social habits, to the fresh conditions in which they find themselves placed. Governments do the same; they adjust the burden of taxation to classes who have become rich, and relieve those which have fallen behind in the race for wealth. Such a contingency as a universal rise of prices is an impossibility, and only less impossible is it that the Government of a country should find itself in the midst of increasing public wealth, and at the same time be in difficulties about raising money to meet the increasing demands of a more highly organized polity. The growth of the revenues of the Government of India, which have more than trebled in forty years, while, owing to a general advance of public prosperity during the same period, the incidence of taxation is more equable and less onerous to the individual than it probably ever has been, is the safest augury by which we can predict that no rise of prices consequent on the enlarged facilities for trade with which a reformed currency will provide the people can prove in any way embarrassing to the Government of India.

Beneficial Effect of Enhanced Prices.

One among other beneficial effects of the increased circulation of money in India is, that by raising prices it enhances the value of the productions of that country all over the world. In some quarters this is not, however, considered an advantage. There are those who consider that it is better for the Indian ryot that he should sell his produce cheap than sell it dear, as the cheaper it is the more he will sell of it. But as cheap and dear are relative terms, such an argument means that the commodities of the exporting country (in this case India) are cheaper than those of the importing country, that is to say, if the advantage in favour of the latter is 25 per cent., the fruit of one hundred and twenty-five days of the labour of the Indian ryot exchanges for the fruit of one hundred days labour on the part of the English workman; and as the exports of India constitute her payments for what she buys abroad, labour for labour, India has to give more for an article of English manufacture than she gets for one of her own. That exchanges on these terms are more beneficial to the exporting country than if the profits on the trade were more equally divided, is an argument that contains its own contradiction. Let it be supposed that an article of Indian production can be sold for £1 4s. at a profit of 1*s.* in England, and that no smaller profit will induce its importation, and that the cost of carriage is 3s., then its cost in India to ensure a profit on its sale in England must be no more than £1. In 1870, £1 sterling was equivalent to Rs. 10, and in 1880 to Rs. 12. If, then, the cost of the article in both years had been in India Rs. 12, it could not have been imported into England in 1870, because its cost would have been equivalent to £1 2s.; but it could have been imported in 1880, when its cost in India was only equal to £1. In this case, the Indian producer was neither better or worse off, by reason of silver having fallen in ten years 20 per cent. He did not sell more of his commodity at the beginning of the period for Rs. 10 than he did at the end for Rs. 12.

The English consumer benefited, for he got in 1880 for £1 what had before cost him £1 2s. Let it next be supposed that the price of the article has risen to Rs. 14. It then ceases to be imported into England; but the Indian producer is no worse off on that account, for the rise in its price shows that the market for the sale of the article has extended; that more purchasers are offering to buy it than before. These additional purchasers may not be Englishmen, but that is of no importance to the producer in India. The latter is benefited by the rise in value, although the former may have to go without the particular commodity. If, however, it is in great request in England, the consumer in the latter country will have to give more for it, he will (other things being equal) have to reduce his expenditure on some other class of goods in order to do so; and if this economy of expenditure is effected in respect of a class of articles which is not produced in India, the latter country attracts to the purchase of her own productions money which formerly had been applied to buying the productions of her neighbours. In any view of the case, a rise of price in Indian productions is advantageous, not injurious to her interests.

Again, let it be supposed that one maund of indigo costs in rupees the equivalent of £20, and that five tons of iron cost £20, and that the equation of exchange is one maund indigo = five tons iron, and that the indigo, when sold in London, fetches £40, and the iron, when sold in India, fetches the equivalent in rupees of £25. If, in consequence of a rise of prices in India, the indigo were to cost more in that market, and the other factors in the calculation remained the same, the proportion between the profits realized by either party to the transaction would be altered. In the first case assumed, England made £20 profit on the sale of the indigo, and India £5 profit on the sale of the iron. In the second case, each would make say £10 and £5 respectively; that is to say, that on the whole transaction India obtained £15 instead of £5 out of the £25 of profit; and although this increase of profit was acquired by way of an increased price for the indigo, it is a real advantage on the whole transaction in favour of India; although if the increased cost of the dye were to have arisen from an increased cost of production, and not from an increased demand for it, the whole of the increased price may not have been clear gain to India to the same extent that it would have been if the cost of production had remained the same. The increase of the proportion of the profit which India in this case has obtained at the expense of England is entirely advantageous to her; and the illustration serves to show that an increase in the prices of commodities in the cheaper and producing country results in their having a higher value abroad, and causes a fairer distribution of the profits of trade between the producing and the consuming country than obtained before.

The Government of the country may in consequence be conducted at an absolutely greater expense, but if its fiscal system is based on sound principles, relatively to the wealth of the country, it need cost no more than before. As was remarked before, the object of a country in producing commodities of a description and quantity not used at home is, that by exporting them they may serve to pay for foreign goods which can either not be produced at all in the country itself or only produced at a greater cost than abroad. No exportation takes place but with a view to making importations cheaper to the consumers in the exporting country than they otherwise would be, and it therefore follows that as long as the people of India continue to increase their productions they are benefiting themselves in two ways, both by giving increased employment to the working classes in the production of the surplus or exported commodities, and by cheapening to the people of the country the goods which are imported in return. And no rise of values in the productions of India, or fall in the purchasing power of her money which may be the result of an increased activity of production and interchange, is otherwise than beneficial to the whole people.

Experience teaches us that in any country whose expanding material prosperity is proved by an increase in the quantity of money in use, its more general diffusion among all classes, and by a developing power to produce, and by variety of production, life is easier, the means of obtaining a livelihood are more numerous, and the avenues to wealth are wider and better planned. Although the money value of the necessaries of life may be absolutely higher than in a former period, it is relatively lower; for while the exchange value of money has diminished, the productions of the national industry are forthcoming in increased quantities, improved in quality, more various in kind, and are more within everybody's means than they were before.

EFFECT OF THE ENGLISH SYSTEM ON INDIAN COMMERCE.

The inhabitants of India possess a civilization which, while it seems to have been arrested during some centuries, preceded that of Europe by many generations. At a time when gold and silver money was but little or at all used on the shores of the Mediterranean, the Indians procured the precious metals from every quarter in which they could sell their exported produce, for conversion into money. They well understood the facilities which the rise of coin provides for the production and exchange of commodities. The economy of coin effected by the use of bills of exchange, the advantages attending the accumulation of the surplus capital of one class of people and its distribution among another for use in trade which constitutes banking, and the insurance against accident of goods in transit, were employed as ordinary commercial expedients in India many generations before they were known in Europe. The antiquity of the commerce of India and the comparative perfection of its methods are quite sufficient to account for the continuous flow of the precious metals from the West to the East from the dawn of history.

The Indians, however, shared the superstition which has been dispelled among educated people only within the last century, that accumulations of gold and silver constitute wealth. The vulgar are slow to realize the fact, that the means of *producing*, not of *purchasing*, the conveniences and luxuries of life really constitute wealth; that gold and silver buried in the ground will not, like seed-corn in a similar situation, germinate and increase. That for all purposes which are connected with wealth, money lying idle in a chest or hidden away in a pot might as well never have been taken out of the mine.

Insecurity of property, the result of the political convulsions to which India was constantly liable, was another cause of the accumulation of treasure in India. The ease with which the precious metals can be concealed or carried about gives them, among people so situated, a peculiar value. It is to these accumulations that India is greatly indebted for the means of enlarging her commerce. Now that the "Pax Britannica" is imposed on the subject powers and people throughout the land, the country has started afresh on the paths of commercial progress with money, the machinery of commerce, supplied by previous generations.

The fiscal legislation of the Indian Government is at once of the most liberal character, and inspired largely with the commercial spirit. A numerous and important class, both in India and in England, may be described, without exaggeration, as considering the development of trade to be the principal argument for the existence of the English in that country. To show no favour to one interest rather than another; to provide means of traffic, facilities for the recovery of debts, for the coinage and use of silver money; to promote the exchange of home and foreign produce,—are objects of administration which are attained with much and increasing success. The people are becoming familiarized with the ways of Western traders, with the principle of association in the production and conveyance of commodities, with the advantages of competition as opposed to combination, of small profits and quick returns distributed among a large number of traders in substitution of large profits obtained at longer intervals by a smaller number. The solvent influence of Western ideas and English legislation on the ancient trade customs of the people of India, no one can fail to perceive on a retrospect of years. One important improvement, the reform of the currency and its assimilation to the systems in use among more civilized nations with which India trades, would be a proper object to engage the solicitude of her rulers, as the following considerations clearly show.

Facility of communication acts as the most cogent inducement to the producers of similar commodities, in places distant from one another, to reduce the prices of their wares to a common level.

Abundance of money alone cannot effect this, for it cannot bring the surplus produce of the country into the towns if the cost of carriage or the absence of roads prohibits conveyance. It is the steamship, the railway, the metalled and bridged roads of this age, that bring the Californian miner and the Indian ryot together. Until the present generation, India was singularly badly off for internal communications. The governors of the country in the last century were too fully occupied in acquiring territory and consolidating our power, and their immediate successors with improving the details of fiscal and political administration to give much attention to this subject; nor were the revenues of the territory or the credit of the British Government equal, until comparatively recent times, to undertaking the expense of bringing remote districts into easy communication with one another. The period when money began to be generally diffused to a more perceptible extent than before, may be said to commence with Lord Dalhousie's tenure of the office of Governor-General of India, which he quitted in 1856. He is justly regarded as the pioneer of civilized communications in India. Under his administration, trunk lines of metalled roads connecting the Eastern, the North-western, and the Western provinces together, running for some thousands of miles in their different courses, were completed. The main lines of now existing railways were sketched out and commenced, and both telegraphic and postal lines were opened out and multiplied, while the attention of local authorities in the interior was constantly directed to perfecting the details of the general plan of improvement. To judge of the effect of these measures on the value of the produce of the interior by bringing it within reach of the money circulating in the towns, one must compare the delay and expense incurred in conveying one hundred tons of goods along unmetalled and unbridged roads, on the backs of bullocks, or in carts drawn by such animals (who necessarily consumed on their journey a weight of food equal to no small portion of their burden), and the cost of carrying the same weight of merchandise by railway, or even along a stone-paved road. The alternative of river transport was full of risk, delay, and uncertainty, and in the interior of the country this mode of conveyance ceases when, in the dry season, the rivers shrink in many places into fordable streams, too shallow to float a barge.

These impediments to the exchange of productions and the circulation of money between not even distant, but adjacent districts restricted the free action of those principles of trade which have been already noticed, and served to intensify the evil effects of combination, as opposed to competition on the commerce of the country. As these are being gradually removed, the habits of thrift and industry, and the commercial spirit of the people are finding vent; the weight being withdrawn, the elasticity of enterprise has found room to play, and the expanding energies of the industrial classes are from time to time setting in motion the machinery of commerce in new centres of population and industry.

A continued multiplication of its home productions which a nation may during a course of years effect, accompanied with an increase in its import of foreign goods for home consumption, indicate an advance in general wealth; since commodities are in the long run neither produced nor imported except at a profit, and those who make the profit must necessarily do so out of an increasing ability on the part of the consuming classes to pay for fresh supplies. No nation can increase its consumption of home and foreign productions unless it be growing richer; the latter condition is an antecedent necessity to the former.

It has been already shown that any increase in the circulation of money can only arise from an increase in the commodities brought into the markets for sale, since money is, from the point of view of commerce, used to no purpose except when effecting exchanges. Any large increase of coin in circulation during a long period of years is therefore proof of a corresponding increase in the amount of goods under exchange. If the contrary were the case, fresh additions to the currency could only be made at a smaller return in labour (in the sense before defined) than was spent on the production of the metal from which they were provided. On such an assumption, consumers in India would have been spending between 250 and 300 per cent. more money than before on the same quantity of commodities. This we know to be inconsistent with the methods of commerce, and, as fact, not to have occurred. Since 1835 prices have improved very considerably, more especially in remote parts of the country never before brought into communication with the principal centres of trade; but in the latter localities, especially during the last ten or fifteen years, violent perturbations of values have become much less frequent, because at the beginning of that period the diffusion of money under the English rule had become fairly complete and commodities have, in consequence, during the period of the great decline of value in silver at the gold valuation, *i.e.* subsequent to 1870, been flowing into the markets in increasing quantities in correspondence with the demand for them expressed by increasing additions to the currency.

Between 1835 and 1855, the Government of India coined only Rs. 685,000,000, of which a little less than a third, or 195,000,000, was a recoinage of existing coin previously issued, but called in at the change of the currency law in 1835. During the period from 1855 to 1882, there have been issued from the Indian mints Rs. 1,910,000,000, of which only 27,500,000 was old money recoined. Putting aside the recoinage of obsolete coins, the people during the first period required therefore a little less than a fourth of the quantity of coin which they required in the latter period for their commerce.

It may here be mentioned that up to 1835 the currency of British India was composed of the coin of the native powers, and that issued from several mints by the East Indian Company in the name of the Emperor of Delhi. In 1835, silver money with the king's head stamped on it first became legal tender in British India.

The condition of the export trade of India affords additional evidence of the capacity of her people to take advantage of the opportunities for gain which the administration puts within their reach. The exports of a country are the measure of its ability to pay for foreign productions, since they are produced and exported both for the purpose of doing so and with the object of providing the home producers with more money than they can obtain by selling their productions in their own country, to invest in fresh enterprises. Hence an expanding import trade is a sure proof of increasing wealth at home. India, whose soil and industries provide all the necessaries and most of the luxuries of life which her inhabitants require, in exporting her productions in exchange for those of foreign countries gets rid of what is more really surplus produce than the exports of another country may be, which are designed to purchase corn, meat, various kinds of food, and other indispensable necessaries. India is in this case disposing of her redundant wealth abroad. The official returns of the exports in the Indian trade, from the year 1855 to 1882 inclusive, estimate their value at within a few thousand pounds of £1,446,000,000, and the same figures show that during the first decade of that period the value of the exports of India was £394,000,000, and during the last decade £657,000,000; the result of a gradual and continuous expand of her trade. Beyond this, no proof is needed of the capacity of the people of India to profit by such an enlargement of their facilities for commerce as this treatise is addressed to recommending.

The prevalence of the custom of trade by barter and the fact that a large part of the agricultural population of India is habitually maintained between seed-time and harvest by advances of food on the part of the grain merchants, to whom the peasantry hypothecate their crops as security for repayment, to some extent account for these large additions to the silver money circulating in India. The new money was necessarily used in making those exchanges which had hitherto been made in kind, and the people, on the other hand, instead of borrowing their food on the credit of the crops on the ground, spent the money thus earned in purchases. But the increased currency was not solely employed in this way, as we know from the fact that this archaic system of trade and subvention is still universally practised, as well as from the vastly increased amount of capital now invested in the carrying trade of the interior of the country in the construction of roads, bridges, and railways, and from the expansion above described of the export trade of India.

It is the increase in the sum of all commodities which have (especially during the last thirty years) been brought for exchange to the Indian markets which has necessitated a corresponding increase in the money in circulation, and which at the same time provides a test of the effect which a diffusion of money, accompanied with enlarged facilities for trade, has upon a people of strong commercial instincts, and justifies the expectation that when the restrictive influence on the foreign trade of India which an exclusive silver currency now exercises is removed, and the £1 sterling becomes the coin in which her produce is sold and her foreign purchases bought, that a fresh start will be made in the development of her internal wealth.

It is but trite to remark that wealth consists in the power to create, and that the inducement to exert that power is found in extended markets; and that the shortest and most convenient road to these objects lies in the use of a common coin, a common measure of value, by both the people of India and their foreign customers.

Exclusive Use of Silver Coin a Restraint on Trade.

It has been frequently remarked that the uncertain value of the silver coin of India in the gold coin of England involves a risk to merchants exporting goods to India of incurring a loss where they expected a profit, from an unexpected fluctuation in the value of the two metals, and that the possibility of such an eventuality has the same effect as the levy of a heavy import duty at the Indian ports.

That such is the case is clear enough. An Indian trader importing English goods has to pay gold for them in Manchester or Sheffield. He has to calculate their price to the Indian purchaser at a sum which will yield the ordinary profit of his business and be sufficient to cover what is known as the loss by exchange, and also to provide against further loss arising from any variation in the relative value of the two metals which may occur before the transaction is completed.

This being the case, the Indian purchaser has to pay a corresponding high price for any goods of this class which he buys. Their sale and their export from Europe consequently fall off. This is one reason among others why a large balance is annually run up against England in the commercial account between her and India which cannot be settled in exports, and must be settled in money. The results of this condition of things have been often and exhaustively discussed, and need no further notice in this place. As the ratio of value between gold and silver narrows, or the rate of exchange becomes more constant under the operation of the scheme now discussed, this restraint on the export of European goods will be reduced; and as, at the same time, the bulk of the currency will not be diminished but rather increased, prices will tend to rise, producers in India will make larger profits and have more money to spend on commodities which in the case assumed will be imported and sold at lower prices than can be accepted now. Thus the use of gold in the manner advocated will stimulate the productions of Western manufactures for the Indian market, and will, by giving employment to increasing quantities of the Indian rupee currency, mitigate any tendency to violent and sudden alterations in the relative value of the two kinds of coin in use in that country.

Accrediting their full force to all these causes combining to arrest a fall in the value of silver against gold, or a rise in the price of commodities against silver, the most cautious of Indian administrators has no need to apprehend the occurrence of any fresh embarrassment in the financial affairs of India from the use of gold exchanging with silver as current coin on the basis of their relative intrinsic value.

LEVY OF REVENUE IN GOLD.

The only course which would effectually terminate the drain on the revenues of India arising from the loss by exchange, which is not likely in the future to be less than Rs. 30,000,000 per annum, is the levy of the public revenue in gold. This could only be done by converting payments now due to be made in silver into their equivalent in gold at the State rate of conversion. It would probably be found expedient to take no step of this kind until the period during which existing arrangements for the levy of the land revenue are in force expires. As the different land revenue settlements come again under revision, some classes of proprietors might be required to pay their revenue at an assessment made in the Indian gold sterling coin. Intermediately other branches of the public revenue which are not periodically readjusted, such as that derived from salt and the sale of opium, might be levied in gold. But before this can be done, gold legal tender money must of necessity be introduced, and the people become familiarized with its use, and the quantity of gold which India can herself annually supply be ascertained by actual experiment. If in the course of a few years the Indian Government could obtain a revenue of only £10,000,000 or £15,000,000 paid in its own gold currency, its principal financial difficulties would disappear.

Nor can a circulation of gold money be maintained with as much regularity as is desirable, unless the Government, which is in the East the principal single source both of demand and supply for coin, assists in promoting its activity. So long as a portion of the public taxes is levied in gold, the same amount of gold will continue to be paid away in purchases, salaries, or the liquidation of drafts on the State treasury, and this force will operate to put gold coin in movement, not only in the principal trading cities, but throughout every administrative circle of towns and villages in the whole Empire. If gold were to leave the country, a constant demand for it as the vehicle for paying several millions sterling in taxes would bring it back again, and the settlement in England of balances due from the Indian Government on account of its public debt and for other purposes, by means of bills drawn against its gold revenues in India, would ensure a continuous disbursement from the local State treasuries of the gold coin, and prevent its accumulation in any particular market.

RESULTS OF THE SCHEME.

The currency system in which gold and silver coins exchange at their true value has, in the particular application recommended in these pages, the advantage of adding largely to the stock of gold coin available for the world's use. It creates a demand for silver to an extent which has been unknown for many years, under a form of bimetallism, which has this attraction for those who are large owners of that metal, that it secures to all men at all times the certainty that their gold or silver in any quantity will always exchange with one another at their actual value, because neither metal will be liable to be affected in its purchasing power by arbitrary or artificial depreciation. No man will fear to use or accumulate for use either kind of coin in any quantity which convenience may dictate; for as one kind of money will always pass at its true rate of value in the other, there can be no loss or gain on the use of either in effecting exchanges of goods. Under such a system, an equilibrium is established between both kinds of currency, without the ruinous expense of recoinage. By giving no advantage to the owners of one metal over those using the other, it leaves existing contracts unaffected; and by maintaining the circulation of a double currency, it secures the employment of gold and silver indifferently in proportions regulated by the volition of the people, and, therefore, in exact correspondence with the requirements of commerce. It leaves the efficiency of silver money unimpaired, and the coinage of rupees unrestricted. It gives the State at once a gold revenue, which may be considerable, and a means of realizing in the course of time the whole of its revenues in gold. It substitutes a firm foundation, upon which its financial administration can be built up in the place of the shifting sand of silver on which that part of its affairs now rests. It places the commercial classes in India in more direct communication with purchasers and producers in foreign countries than can be contrived by any other means. By promoting the exchange of goods and the expansion of trade, it becomes an aid to the people of India in their efforts to enrich themselves and thereby strengthens equally the commercial and political interests which attach the Dependency to the paramount Power. By making the Indian currency a machine for certifying the value of the precious metals and for securing their exchange at their true value for commodities, it gives to the Indian trader, whether purchaser or producer, an advantage over competitors in many other countries, and serves to attract capital to India for investment by the security it affords that the returns will be obtained in coin exempt from depreciation by artificial causes. So far as this scheme would affect the mass of the population, its employment would act as a constant stimulus to production, and operate to diffuse coined money in increasing quantities among the largest possible number of people. It would tend to discourage the customs of sale by barter, of purchase on long credits and payment in kind. Nothing in the fiscal or commercial condition of India offers any serious difficulty to the circulation of money on the terms herein discussed. Against the public advantage and the removal of restraints on trade, which this reform of the currency effects, there is no set-off in any way mischievous or injurious which it is likely to originate. For all the evils arising out of "the silver question," it is the single remedy which can be applied in India.

THE END.

A LIST OF

KEGAN PAUL, TRENCH & CO.'S PUBLICATIONS.

1, *Paternoster Square,*
London.

A LIST OF

KEGAN PAUL, TRENCH & CO.'S PUBLICATIONS.

CONTENTS.

GENERAL LITERATURE.

ADAMSON, H. T., B.D.—**The Truth as it is in Jesus.** Crown 8vo, 8*s.* 6*d.*

The Three Sevens. Crown 8vo, 5*s.* 6*d.*

The Millennium; or, the Mystery of God Finished. Crown 8vo, 6*s.*

A. K. H. B.—**From a Quiet Place.** A New Volume of Sermons. Crown 8vo, 5*s.*

ALLEN, Rev. R., M.A.—**Abraham: his Life, Times, and Travels,** 3800 years ago. With Map. Second Edition. Post 8vo, 6*s.*

ALLIES, T. W., M.A.—**Per Crucem ad Lucem.** The Result of a Life. 2 vols. Demy 8vo, 25*s.*

A Life's Decision. Crown 8vo, 7*s.* 6*d.*

AMOS, Professor Sheldon.—**The History and Principles of the Civil Law of Rome.** An aid to the Study of Scientific and Comparative Jurisprudence. Demy 8vo. 16*s.*

ANDERDON, Rev. W. H.—**Fasti Apostolici;** a Chronology of the Years between the Ascension of our Lord and the Martyrdom of SS. Peter and Paul. Second Edition. Crown 8vo, 2*s.* 6*d.*

Evenings with the Saints. Crown 8vo, 5*s.*

ARMSTRONG, Richard A., B.A.—**Latter-Day Teachers.** Six Lectures. Small crown 8vo, 2*s.* 6*d.*

AUBERTIN, J. J.—**A Flight to Mexico.** With Seven full-page Illustrations and a Railway Map of Mexico. Crown 8vo, *7s. 6d.*

BADGER, George Percy, D.C.L.—**An English-Arabic Lexicon.** In which the equivalent for English Words and Idiomatic Sentences are rendered into literary and colloquial Arabic. Royal 4to, *£9 9s.*

BAGEHOT, Walter.—**The English Constitution.** Third Edition. Crown 8vo, *7s. 6d.*

Lombard Street. A Description of the Money Market. Eighth Edition. Crown 8vo, *7s. 6d.*

Some Articles on the Depreciation of Silver, and Topics connected with it. Demy 8vo, *5s.*

BAGENAL, Philip H.—**The American-Irish and their Influence on Irish Politics.** Crown 8vo, *5s.*

BAGOT, Alan, C.E.—**Accidents in Mines: their Causes and Prevention.** Crown 8vo, *6s.*

The Principles of Colliery Ventilation. Second Edition, greatly enlarged. Crown 8vo, *5s.*

BAKER, Sir Sherston, Bart.—**The Laws relating to Quarantine.** Crown 8vo, *12s. 6d.*

BALDWIN, Capt. J. H.—**The Large and Small Game of Bengal and the North-Western Provinces of India.** With 18 Illustrations. New and Cheaper Edition. Small 4to, *10s. 6d.*

BALLIN, Ada S. and F. L.—**A Hebrew Grammar.** With Exercises selected from the Bible. Crown 8vo, *7s. 6d.*

BARCLAY, Edgar.—**Mountain Life in Algeria.** With numerous Illustrations by Photogravure. Crown 4to, *16s.*

BARLOW, James H.—**The Ultimatum of Pessimism.** An Ethical Study. Demy 8vo, *6s.*

BARNES, William.—**Outlines of Redecraft (Logic).** With English Wording. Crown 8vo, *3s.*

BAUR, Ferdinand, Dr. Ph.—**A Philological Introduction to Greek and Latin for Students.** Translated and adapted from the German, by C. KEGAN PAUL, M.A., and E. D. STONE, M.A. Third Edition. Crown 8vo, *6s.*

BELLARS, Rev. W.—**The Testimony of Conscience to the Truth and Divine Origin of the Christian Revelation.** Burney Prize Essay. Small crown 8vo, *3s. 6d.*

BELLINGHAM, Henry, M.P.—**Social Aspects of Catholicism and Protestantism in their Civil Bearing upon Nations.** Translated and adapted from the French of M. le BARON DE HAULLEVILLE. With a preface by His Eminence CARDINAL MANNING. Second and Cheaper Edition. Crown 8vo, *3s. 6d.*

BELLINGHAM H. Belsches Graham.—**Ups and Downs of Spanish Travel.** Second Edition. Crown 8vo. 5*s.*

BENN, Alfred W.—**The Greek Philosophers.** 2 vols. Demy 8vo, 28*s.*

BENT, J. Theodore.—**Genoa: How the Republic Rose and Fell.** With 18 Illustrations. Demy 8vo, 18*s.*

BLOOMFIELD, The Lady.—**Reminiscences of Court and Diplomatic Life.** New and Cheaper Edition. With Frontispiece. Crown 8vo, 6*s.*

BLUNT, The Ven. Archdeacon.—**The Divine Patriot, and other Sermons.** Preached in Scarborough and in Cannes. New and Cheaper Edition. Crown 8vo, 4*s.* 6*d.*

BLUNT, Wilfred S.—**The Future of Islam.** Crown 8vo, 6*s.*

BONWICK, J., F.R.G.S.—**Pyramid Facts and Fancies.** Crown 8vo, 5*s.*

BOUVERIE-PUSEY, S. E. B.—**Permanence and Evolution.** An Inquiry into the Supposed Mutability of Animal Types. Crown 8vo, 5*s.*

BOWEN, H. C., M.A.—**Studies in English.** For the use of Modern Schools. Third Edition. Small crown 8vo, 1*s.* 6*d.*

English Grammar for Beginners. Fcap. 8vo, 1*s.*

BRADLEY, F. H.—**The Principles of Logic.** Demy 8vo, 16*s.*

BRIDGETT, Rev. T. E.—**History of the Holy Eucharist in Great Britain.** 2 vols. Demy 8vo, 18*s.*

BRODRICK, the Hon. G. C.—**Political Studies.** Demy 8vo, 14*s.*

BROOKE, Rev. S. A.—**Life and Letters of the Late Rev. F. W. Robertson, M.A.** Edited by.

I. Uniform with Robertson's Sermons. 2 vols. With Steel Portrait. 7*s.* 6*d.*
II. Library Edition. With Portrait. 8vo, 12*s.*
III. A Popular Edition. In 1 vol., 8vo, 6*s.*

The Fight of Faith. Sermons preached on various occasions. Fifth Edition. Crown 8vo, 7*s.* 6*d.*

The Spirit of the Christian Life. New and Cheaper Edition. Crown 8vo, 5*s.*

Theology in the English Poets.—Cowper, Coleridge, Wordsworth, and Burns. Fifth and Cheaper Edition. Post 8vo, 5*s.*

Christ in Modern Life. Sixteenth and Cheaper Edition. Crown 8vo, 5*s.*

Sermons. First Series. Thirteenth and Cheaper Edition. Crown 8vo, 5*s.*

Sermons. Second Series. Sixth and Cheaper Edition. Crown 8vo, 5*s.*

BROWN, Rev. J. Baldwin, B.A.—**The Higher Life.** Its Reality, Experience, and Destiny. Fifth Edition. Crown 8vo, 5*s.*

Doctrine of Annihilation in the Light of the Gospel of Love. Five Discourses. Fourth Edition. Crown 8vo, 2*s.* 6*d.*

The Christian Policy of Life. A Book for Young Men of Business. Third Edition. Crown 8vo, 3*s.* 6*d.*

BROWN, S. Borton, B.A.—**The Fire Baptism of all Flesh;** or, the Coming Spiritual Crisis of the Dispensation. Crown 8vo, 6*s.*

BROWNBILL, John.—**Principles of English Canon Law.** Part I. General Introduction. Crown 8vo, 6*s.*

BROWNE, W. R.—**The Inspiration of the New Testament.** With a Preface by the Rev. J. P. NORRIS, D.D. Fcap. 8vo, 2*s.* 6*d.*

BURTON, Mrs. Richard.—**The Inner Life of Syria, Palestine, and the Holy Land.** Cheaper Edition in one volume. Large post 8vo. 7*s.* 6*d.*

BUSBECQ, Ogier Ghiselin de.—**His Life and Letters.** By CHARLES THORNTON FORSTER, M.A., and F. H. BLACKBURNE DANIELL, M.A. 2 vols. With Frontispieces. Demy 8vo, 24*s.*

CARPENTER, W. B., LL.D., M.D., F.R.S., etc.—**The Principles of Mental Physiology.** With their Applications to the Training and Discipline of the Mind, and the Study of its Morbid Conditions. Illustrated. Sixth Edition. 8vo, 12*s.*

CERVANTES.—**The Ingenious Knight Don Quixote de la Mancha.** A New Translation from the Originals of 1605 and 1608. By A. J. DUFFIELD. With Notes. 3 vols. Demy 8vo, 42*s.*

Journey to Parnassus. Spanish Text, with Translation into English Tercets, Preface, and Illustrative Notes, by JAMES Y. GIBSON. Crown 8vo, 12*s.*

CHEYNE, Rev. T. K.—**The Prophecies of Isaiah.** Translated with Critical Notes and Dissertations. 2 vols. Second Edition. Demy 8vo, 25*s.*

CLAIRAUT.—**Elements of Geometry.** Translated by Dr. KAINES. With 145 Figures. Crown 8vo, 4*s.* 6*d.*

CLAYDEN, P. W.—**England under Lord Beaconsfield.** The Political History of the Last Six Years, from the end of 1873 to the beginning of 1880. Second Edition, with Index and continuation to March, 1880. Demy 8vo, 16*s.*

Samuel Sharpe. Egyptologist and Translator of the Bible. Crown 8vo, 6*s.*

CLIFFORD, Samuel.—**What Think Ye of Christ?** Crown 8vo. 6*s.*

CLODD, Edward, F.R.A.S.—**The Childhood of the World:** a Simple Account of Man in Early Times. Seventh Edition. Crown 8vo, 3*s.*

A Special Edition for Schools. 1*s.*

CLOD, Edward, F.R.A.S.—continued.

The Childhood of Religions. Including a Simple Account of the Birth and Growth of Myths and Legends. Eighth Thousand. Crown 8vo, 5*s.*

A Special Edition for Schools. 1*s.* 6*d.*

Jesus of Nazareth. With a brief sketch of Jewish History to the Time of His Birth. Small crown 8vo, 6*s.*

COGHLAN, J. Cole, D.D.—**The Modern Pharisee and other Sermons.** Edited by the Very Rev. H. H. DICKINSON, D.D., Dean of Chapel Royal, Dublin. New and Cheaper Edition. Crown 8vo, 7*s.* 6*d.*

COLERIDGE, Sara.—**Memoir and Letters of Sara Coleridge.** Edited by her Daughter. With Index. Cheap Edition. With Portrait. 7*s.* 6*d.*

Collects Exemplified. Being Illustrations from the Old and New Testaments of the Collects for the Sundays after Trinity. By the Author of "A Commentary on the Epistles and Gospels." Edited by the Rev. JOSEPH JACKSON. Crown 8vo, 5*s.*

CONNELL, A. K.—**Discontent and Danger in India.** Small crown 8vo, 3*s.* 6*d.*

The Economic Revolution of India. Crown 8vo, 5*s.*

CORY, William.—**A Guide to Modern English History.** Part I. —MDCCCXV.-MDCCCXXX. Demy 8vo, 9*s.* Part II.—MDCCCXXX.-MDCCCXXXV., 15*s.*

COTTERILL, H. B.—**An Introduction to the Study of Poetry.** Crown 8vo, 7*s.* 6*d.*

COX, Rev. Sir George W., M.A., Bart.—**A History of Greece from the Earliest Period to the end of the Persian War.** New Edition. 2 vols. Demy 8vo, 36*s.*

The Mythology of the Aryan Nations. New Edition. Demy 8vo, 16*s.*

Tales of Ancient Greece. New Edition. Small crown 8vo, 6*s.*

A Manual of Mythology in the form of Question and Answer. New Edition. Fcap. 8vo, 3*s.*

An Introduction to the Science of Comparative Mythology and Folk-Lore. Second Edition. Crown 8vo. 7*s.* 6*d.*

COX, Rev. Sir G. W., M.A., Bart., and JONES, Eustace Hinton.—**Popular Romances of the Middle Ages.** Second Edition, in 1 vol. Crown 8vo, 6*s.*

COX, Rev. Samuel, D.D.—**Salvator Mundi**; or, Is Christ the Saviour of all Men? Eighth Edition. Crown 8vo, 5*s.*

The Genesis of Evil, and other Sermons, mainly expository. Third Edition. Crown 8vo, 6*s.*

COX, Rev. Samuel, D.D.—continued.

A Commentary on the Book of Job. With a Translation. Demy 8vo, 15*s.*

The Larger Hope. A Sequel to "Salvator Mundi." 16mo, 1*s.*

CRAVEN, Mrs.—**A Year's Meditations.** Crown 8vo, 6*s.*

CRAWFURD, Oswald.—**Portugal, Old and New.** With Illustrations and Maps. New and Cheaper Edition. Crown 8vo, 6*s.*

CROZIER, John Beattie, M.B.—**The Religion of the Future.** Crown 8vo, 6*s.*

Cyclopædia of Common Things. Edited by the Rev. Sir GEORGE W. COX, Bart., M.A. With 500 Illustrations. Third Edition. Large post 8vo, 7*s.* 6*d.*

DAVIDSON, Rev. Samuel, D.D., LL.D.—**Canon of the Bible:** Its Formation, History, and Fluctuations. Third and Revised Edition. Small crown 8vo, 5*s.*

The Doctrine of Last Things contained in the New Testament compared with the Notions of the Jews and the Statements of Church Creeds. Small crown 8vo, 3*s.* 6*d.*

DAVIDSON, Thomas.—**The Parthenon Frieze,** and other Essays. Crown 8vo, 6*s.*

DAWSON, Geo., M.A. **Prayers, with a Discourse on Prayer.** Edited by his Wife. Eighth Edition. Crown 8vo, 6*s.*

Sermons on Disputed Points and Special Occasions. Edited by his Wife. Fourth Edition. Crown 8vo, 6*s.*

Sermons on Daily Life and Duty. Edited by his Wife. Fourth Edition. Crown 8vo, 6*s.*

The Authentic Gospel. A New Volume of Sermons. Edited by GEORGE ST. CLAIR. Third Edition. Crown 8vo, 6*s.*

Three Books of God: Nature, History, and Scripture. Sermons edited by GEORGE ST. CLAIR. Crown 8vo, 6*s.*

DE JONCOURT, Madame Marie.—**Wholesome Cookery.** Crown 8vo, 3*s.* 6*d.*

DE LONG, Lieut. Com. G. W.—**The Voyage of the Jeannette.** The Ship and Ice Journals of. Edited by his Wife, EMMA DE LONG. With Portraits, Maps, and many Illustrations on wood and stone. 2 vols. Demy 8vo. 36*s.*

DESPREZ, Phillip S., B.D.—**Daniel and John;** or, the Apocalypse of the Old and that of the New Testament. Demy 8vo, 12*s.*

DOWDEN, Edward, LL.D.—**Shakspere:** a Critical Study of his Mind and Art. Sixth Edition. Post 8vo, 12*s.*

Studies in Literature, 1789–1877. Second and Cheaper Edition. Large post 8vo, 6*s.*

DUFFIELD, A. J.—**Don Quixote: his Critics and Commentators.** With a brief account of the minor works of MIGUEL DE CERVANTES SAAVEDRA, and a statement of the aim and end of the greatest of them all. A handy book for general readers. Crown 8vo, 3*s.* 6*d.*

DU MONCEL, Count.—**The Telephone, the Microphone, and the Phonograph.** With 74 Illustrations. Second Edition. Small crown 8vo, 5*s.*

EDGEWORTH, F. Y.—**Mathematical Psychics.** An Essay on the Application of Mathematics to Social Science. Demy 8vo, 7*s.* 6*d.*

Educational Code of the Prussian Nation, in its Present Form. In accordance with the Decisions of the Common Provincial Law, and with those of Recent Legislation. Crown 8vo, 2*s.* 6*d.*

Education Library. Edited by PHILIP MAGNUS:—

An Introduction to the History of Educational Theories. By OSCAR BROWNING, M.A. Second Edition. 3*s.* 6*d.*

Old Greek Education. By the Rev. Prof. MAHAFFY, M.A. 3*s.* 6*d.*

School Management. Including a general view of the work of Education, Organization and Discipline. By JOSEPH LANDON. Second Edition. 6*s.*

Eighteenth Century Essays. Selected and Edited by AUSTIN DOBSON. With a Miniature Frontispiece by R. Caldecott. Parchment Library Edition, 6*s.*; vellum, 7*s.* 6*d.*

ELSDALE, Henry.—**Studies in Tennyson's Idylls.** Crown 8vo, 5*s.*

ELYOT, Sir Thomas.—**The Boke named the Gouernour.** Edited from the First Edition of 1531 by HENRY HERBERT STEPHEN CROFT, M.A., Barrister-at-Law. With Portraits of Sir Thomas and Lady Elyot, copied by permission of her Majesty from Holbein's Original Drawings at Windsor Castle. 2 vols. Fcap. 4to, 50*s.*

Enoch the Prophet. The Book of. Archbishop LAURENCE'S Translation, with an Introduction by the Author of "The Evolution of Christianity." Crown 8vo, 5*s.*

Eranus. A Collection of Exercises in the Alcaic and Sapphic Metres. Edited by F. W. CORNISH, Assistant Master at Eton. Crown 8vo, 2*s.*

EVANS, Mark.—**The Story of Our Father's Love,** told to Children. Sixth and Cheaper Edition. With Four Illustrations. Fcap. 8vo, 1*s.* 6*d.*

EVANS, Mark—continued.

A Book of Common Prayer and Worship for Household Use, compiled exclusively from the Holy Scriptures. Second Edition. Fcap. 8vo, 1*s.*

The Gospel of Home Life. Crown 8vo, 4*s.* 6*d.*

The King's Story-Book. In Three Parts. Fcap. 8vo, 1*s.* 6*d.* each.

*** Parts I. and II. with Eight Illustrations and Two Picture Maps, now ready.

"Fan Kwae" at Canton before Treaty Days 1825-1844. By an old Resident. With Frontispiece. Crown 8vo, 5*s.*

FLECKER, Rev. Eliezer.—**Scripture Onomatology.** Being Critical Notes on the Septuagint and other versions. Crown 8vo, 3*s.* 6*d.*

FLOREDICE, W. H.—**A Month among the Mere Irish.** Small crown 8vo, 5*s.*

GARDINER, Samuel R., and J. BASS MULLINGER, M.A.—**Introduction to the Study of English History.** Large Crown 8vo, 9*s.*

GARDNER, Dorsey.—**Quatre Bras, Ligny, and Waterloo.** A Narrative of the Campaign in Belgium, 1815. With Maps and Plans. Demy 8vo, 16*s.*

Genesis in Advance of Present Science. A Critical Investigation of Chapters I.–IX. By a Septuagenarian Beneficed Presbyter. Demy 8vo. 10*s.* 6*d.*

GENNA, E.—**Irresponsible Philanthropists.** Being some Chapters on the Employment of Gentlewomen. Small crown 8vo, 2*s.* 6*d.*

GEORGE, Henry.—**Progress and Poverty** : An Inquiry into the Causes of Industrial Depressions, and of Increase of Want with Increase of Wealth. The Remedy. Second Edition. Post 8vo, 7*s.* 6*d.* Also a Cheap Edition. Limp cloth, 1*s.* 6*d.* Paper covers, 1*s.*

GIBSON, James Y.—**Journey to Parnassus.** Composed by MIGUEL DE CERVANTES SAAVEDRA. Spanish Text, with Translation into English Tercets, Preface, and Illustrative Notes, by. Crown 8vo, 12*s.*

Glossary of Terms and Phrases. Edited by the Rev. H. PERCY SMITH and others. Medium 8vo, 12*s.*

GLOVER, F., M.A.—**Exempla Latina.** A First Construing Book, with Short Notes, Lexicon, and an Introduction to the Analysis of Sentences. Fcap. 8vo, 2*s.*

GOLDSMID, Sir Francis Henry, Bart., Q.C., M.P.—**Memoir of.** With Portrait. Second Edition, Revised. Crown 8vo, 6*s.*

GOODENOUGH, Commodore J. G.—**Memoir of, with Extracts from his Letters and Journals.** Edited by his Widow. With Steel Engraved Portrait. Square 8vo, 5*s*.

⁂ Also a Library Edition with Maps, Woodcuts, and Steel Engraved Portrait. Square post 8vo, 14*s*.

GOSSE, Edmund W.—**Studies in the Literature of Northern Europe.** With a Frontispiece designed and etched by Alma Tadema. New and Cheaper Edition. Large crown 8vo, 6*s*.

Seventeenth Century Studies. A Contribution to the History of English Poetry. Demy 8vo, 10*s*. 6*d*.

GOULD, Rev. S. Baring, M.A.—**Germany, Present and Past.** New and Cheaper Edition. Large crown 8vo, 7*s*. 6*d*.

GOWAN, Major Walter E.—**A. Ivanoff's Russian Grammar.** (16th Edition.) Translated, enlarged, and arranged for use of Students of the Russian Language. Demy 8vo, 6*s*.

GOWER, Lord Ronald. **My Reminiscences.** Second Edition. 2 vols. With Frontispieces. Demy 8vo, 30*s*.

GRAHAM, William, M.A.—**The Creed of Science,** Religious, Moral, and Social. Demy 8vo, 6*s*.

GRIFFITH, Thomas, A.M.—**The Gospel of the Divine Life:** a Study of the Fourth Evangelist. Demy 8vo, 14*s*.

GRIMLEY, Rev. H. N., M.A.—**Tremadoc Sermons, chiefly on the Spiritual Body, the Unseen World, and the Divine Humanity.** Third Edition. Crown 8vo, 6*s*.

HAECKEL, Prof. Ernst.—**The History of Creation.** Translation revised by Professor E. RAY LANKESTER, M.A., F.R.S. With Coloured Plates and Genealogical Trees of the various groups of both Plants and Animals. 2 vols. Third Edition. Post 8vo, 32*s*.

The History of the Evolution of Man. With numerous Illustrations. 2 vols. Post 8vo, 32*s*.

A Visit to Ceylon. Post 8vo, 7*s*. 6*d*.

Freedom in Science and Teaching. With a Prefatory Note by T. H. HUXLEY, F.R.S. Crown 8vo, 5*s*.

HALF-CROWN SERIES :—

A Lost Love. By ANNA C. OGLE [Ashford Owen].

Sister Dora : a Biography. By MARGARET LONSDALE.

True Words for Brave Men : a Book for Soldiers and Sailors. By the late CHARLES KINGSLEY.

An Inland Voyage. By R. L. STEVENSON.

Travels with a Donkey. By R. L. STEVENSON.

HALF-CROWN SERIES—*continued.*

Notes of Travel: being Extracts from the Journals of Count VON MOLTKE.

English Sonnets. Collected and Arranged by J. DENNIS.

London Lyrics. By F. LOCKER.

Home Songs for Quiet Hours. By the Rev. Canon R. H. BAYNES.

HAWEIS, Rev. H. R., M.A.—**Current Coin.** Materialism—The Devil—Crime—Drunkenness—Pauperism—Emotion—Recreation—The Sabbath. Fifth and Cheaper Edition. Crown 8vo, 5*s.*

Arrows in the Air. Fifth and Cheaper Edition. Crown 8vo, 5*s.*

Speech in Season. Fifth and Cheaper Edition. Crown 8vo, 5*s.*

Thoughts for the Times. Thirteenth and Cheaper Edition. Crown 8vo, 5*s.*

Unsectarian Family Prayers. New and Cheaper Edition. Fcap. 8vo, 1*s.* 6*d.*

HAWKINS, Edwards Comerford.—**Spirit and Form.** Sermons preached in the Parish Church of Leatherhead. Crown 8vo, 6*s.*

HAWTHORNE, Nathaniel.—**Works.** Complete in Twelve Volumes. Large post 8vo, 7*s.* 6*d.* each volume.

VOL. I. TWICE-TOLD TALES.
II. MOSSES FROM AN OLD MANSE.
III. THE HOUSE OF THE SEVEN GABLES, AND THE SNOW IMAGE.
IV. THE WONDERBOOK, TANGLEWOOD TALES, AND GRANDFATHER'S CHAIR.
V. THE SCARLET LETTER, AND THE BLITHEDALE ROMANCE.
VI. THE MARBLE FAUN. [Transformation.]
VII. } VIII. } OUR OLD HOME, AND ENGLISH NOTE-BOOKS.
IX. AMERICAN NOTE-BOOKS.
X. FRENCH AND ITALIAN NOTE-BOOKS.
XI. SEPTIMIUS FELTON, THE DOLLIVER ROMANCE, FANSHAWE, AND, IN AN APPENDIX, THE ANCESTRAL FOOTSTEP.
XII. TALES AND ESSAYS, AND OTHER PAPERS, WITH A BIOGRAPHICAL SKETCH OF HAWTHORNE.

HAYES, A. H., Junr.—**New Colorado, and the Santa Fé Trail.** With Map and 60 Illustrations. Crown 8vo, 9*s.*

HENNESSY, Sir John Pope.—**Ralegh in Ireland.** With his Letters on Irish Affairs and some Contemporary Documents. Large crown 8vo, printed on hand-made paper, parchment, 10*s.* 6*d.*

HENRY, Philip.—**Diaries and Letters of.** Edited by MATTHEW HENRY LEE, M.A. Large crown 8vo, 7*s.* 6*d.*

HIDE, Albert.—**The Age to Come.** Small crown 8vo, 2*s.* 6*d.*

HIME, Major H. W. L., R.A.—**Wagnerism: A Protest.** Crown 8vo, 2*s.* 6*d.*

HINTON, J.—**Life and Letters.** Edited by ELLICE HOPKINS, with an Introduction by Sir W. W. GULL, Bart., and Portrait engraved on Steel by C. H. Jeens. Fourth Edition. Crown 8vo, 8*s.* 6*d.*

The Mystery of Pain. New Edition. Fcap. 8vo, 1*s.*

HOLTHAM, E. G.—**Eight Years in Japan, 1873-1881.** Work, Travel, and Recreation. With three maps. Large crown 8vo, 9*s.*

HOOPER, Mary.—**Little Dinners: How to Serve them with Elegance and Economy.** Seventeenth Edition. Crown 8vo, 2*s.* 6*d.*

Cookery for Invalids, Persons of Delicate Digestion, and Children. Third Edition. Crown 8vo, 2*s.* 6*d.*

Every-Day Meals. Being Economical and Wholesome Recipes for Breakfast, Luncheon, and Supper. Fifth Edition. Crown 8vo, 2*s.* 6*d.*

HOPKINS, Ellice.—**Life and Letters of James Hinton,** with an Introduction by Sir W. W. GULL, Bart., and Portrait engraved on Steel by C. H. Jeens. Fourth Edition. Crown 8vo, 8*s.* 6*d.*

Work amongst Working Men. Fourth edition. Crown 8vo, 3*s.* 6*d.*

HOSPITALIER, E.—**The Modern Applications of Electricity.** Translated and Enlarged by JULIUS MAIER, Ph.D. 2 vols. With numerous Illustrations. Demy 8vo, 12*s.* 6*d.* each volume.

VOL. I.—Electric Generators, Electric Light.

VOL. II.—Telephone: Various Applications: Electrical Transmission of Energy.

Household Readings on Prophecy. By a Layman. Small crown 8vo, 3*s.* 6*d.*

HUGHES, Henry.—**The Redemption of the World.** Crown 8vo, 3*s.* 6*d.*

HUNTINGFORD, Rev. E., D.C.L.—**The Apocalypse.** With a Commentary and Introductory Essay. Demy 8vo, 9*s.*

HUTTON, Arthur, M.A.—**The Anglican Ministry:** Its Nature and Value in relation to the Catholic Priesthood. With a Preface by His Eminence CARDINAL NEWMAN. Demy 8vo, 14*s.*

HUTTON, Rev. C. F.—**Unconscious Testimony;** or, the Silent Witness of the Hebrew to the Truth of the Historical Scriptures. Crown 8vo, 2*s.* 6*d.*

IM THURN, Everard F.—**Among the Indians of British Guiana.** Being Sketches, chiefly anthropologic, from the Interior of British Guiana. With numerous Illustrations. Demy 8vo.

JENKINS, E., and RAYMOND, J.—**The Architect's Legal Handbook.** Third Edition, Revised. Crown 8vo, 6*s*.

JENKINS, Rev. R. C., M.A.—**The Privilege of Peter,** and the Claims of the Roman Church confronted with the Scriptures, the Councils, and the Testimony of the Popes themselves. Fcap. 8vo, 3*s*. 6*d*.

JERVIS, Rev. W. Henley.—**The Gallican Church and the Revolution.** A Sequel to the History of the Church of France, from the Concordat of Bologna to the Revolution. Demy 8vo, 18*s*.

JOEL, L.—**A Consul's Manual and Shipowner's and Shipmaster's Practical Guide in their Transactions Abroad.** With Definitions of Nautical, Mercantile, and Legal Terms; a Glossary of Mercantile Terms in English, French, German, Italian, and Spanish; Tables of the Money, Weights, and Measures of the Principal Commercial Nations and their Equivalents in British Standards; and Forms of Consular and Notarial Acts. Demy 8vo, 12*s*.

JOHNSTONE, C. F., M.A.—**Historical Abstracts:** being Outlines of the History of some of the less known States of Europe. Crown 8vo, 7*s*. 6*d*.

JOLLY, William, F.R.S.E., etc.—**The Life of John Duncan, Scotch Weaver and Botanist.** With Sketches of his Friends and Notices of his Times. Second Edition. Large crown 8vo, with etched portrait, 9*s*.

JONES, C. A.—**The Foreign Freaks of Five Friends.** With 30 Illustrations. Crown 8vo, 6*s*.

JOYCE, P. W., LL.D., etc.—**Old Celtic Romances.** Translated from the Gaelic. Crown 8vo, 7*s*. 6*d*.

JOYNES, J. L.—**The Adventures of a Tourist in Ireland.** Second edition. Small crown 8vo, 2*s*. 6*d*.

KAUFMANN, Rev. M., B.A.—**Socialism:** its Nature, its Dangers, and its Remedies considered. Crown 8vo, 7*s*. 6*d*.

Utopias; or, Schemes of Social Improvement, from Sir Thomas More to Karl Marx. Crown 8vo, 5*s*.

KAY, Joseph.—**Free Trade in Land.** Edited by his Widow. With Preface by the Right Hon. JOHN BRIGHT, M.P. Sixth Edition. Crown 8vo, 5*s*.

KEMPIS, Thomas à.—**Of the Imitation of Christ.** Parchment Library Edition, 6*s*.; or vellum, 7*s*. 6*d*. The Red Line Edition, fcap. 8vo, red edges, 2*s*. 6*d*. The Cabinet Edition, small 8vo, cloth limp, 1*s*.; cloth boards, red edges, 1*s*. 6*d*. The Miniature Edition, red edges, 32mo, 1*s*.

*** All the above Editions may be had in various extra bindings.

KENT, C.—**Corona Catholica ad Petri successoris Pedes Oblata. De Summi Pontificis Leonis XIII. Assumptione Epigramma.** In Quinquaginta Linguis. Fcap. 4to, 15*s*.

KETTLEWELL, Rev. S.—**Thomas à Kempis and the Brothers of Common Life.** 2 vols. With Frontispieces. Demy 8vo, 30*s*.

KIDD, Joseph, M.D.—**The Laws of Therapeutics**; or, the Science and Art of Medicine. Second Edition. Crown 8vo, 6*s*.

KINGSFORD, Anna, M.D.—**The Perfect Way in Diet.** A Treatise advocating a Return to the Natural and Ancient Food of our Race. Small crown 8vo, 2*s*.

KINGSLEY, Charles, M.A.—**Letters and Memories of his Life.** Edited by his Wife. With two Steel Engraved Portraits, and Vignettes on Wood. Thirteenth Cabinet Edition. 2 vols. Crown 8vo, 12*s*.

*** Also a New and Condensed Edition, in one volume. With Portrait. Crown 8vo, 6*s*.

All Saints' Day, and other Sermons. Also a new and condensed Edition in one volume, with Portrait. Crown 8vo, 6*s*. Edited by the Rev. W. HARRISON. Third Edition. Crown 8vo, 7*s*. 6*d*.

True Words for Brave Men. A Book for Soldiers' and Sailors' Libraries. Tenth Edition. Crown 8vo, 2*s*. 6*d*.

KNOX, Alexander A.—**The New Playground**; or, Wanderings in Algeria. New and cheaper edition. Large crown 8vo, 6*s*.

LANDON Joseph.—**School Management**; Including a General View of the Work of Education, Organization, and Discipline. Second Edition. Crown 8vo, 6*s*.

LAURIE, S. S.—**The Training of Teachers,** and other Educational Papers. Crown 8vo, 7*s*. 6*d*.

LEE, Rev. F. G., D.C.L.—**The Other World**; or, Glimpses of the Supernatural. 2 vols. A New Edition. Crown 8vo, 15*s*.

Letters from a Young Emigrant in Manitoba. Second Edition. Small crown 8vo, 3*s*. 6*d*.

LEWIS, Edward Dillon.—**A Draft Code of Criminal Law and Procedure.** Demy 8vo, 21*s*.

LILLIE, Arthur, M.R.A.S.—**The Popular Life of Buddha.** Containing an Answer to the Hibbert Lectures of 1881. With Illustrations. Crown 8vo, 6*s*.

LINDSAY, W. Lauder, M.D.—**Mind in the Lower Animals in Health and Disease.** 2 vols. Demy 8vo, 32*s*.

Vol. I.—Mind in Health. Vol. II.—Mind in Disease.

LLOYD, Walter.—**The Hope of the World**: An Essay on Universal Redemption. Crown 8vo, 5*s*.

LONSDALE, Margaret.—**Sister Dora**: a Biography. With Portrait. Twenty-fifth Edition. Crown 8vo, 2*s*. 6*d*.

LOWDER, Charles.—**A Biography.** By the Author of "St. Teresa." New and Cheaper Edition. Crown 8vo. With Portrait. 3*s*. 6*d*.

LYTTON, Edward Bulwer, Lord.—**Life, Letters and Literary Remains.** By his Son, The EARL OF LYTTON. With Portraits, Illustrations and Facsimiles. Demy 8vo.
[Vols. I. and II. just ready.

MACHIAVELLI, Niccolò.—**Discourses on the First Decade of Titus Livius.** Translated from the Italian by NINIAN HILL THOMSON, M.A. Large crown 8vo, 12*s.*

The Prince. Translated from the Italian by N. H. T. Small crown 8vo, printed on hand-made paper, bevelled boards, 6*s.*

MACKENZIE, Alexander.—**How India is Governed.** Being an Account of England's Work in India. Small crown 8vo, 2*s.*

MACNAUGHT, Rev. John.—**Cœna Domini:** An Essay on the Lord's Supper, its Primitive Institution, Apostolic Uses, and Subsequent History. Demy 8vo, 14*s.*

MACWALTER, Rev. G. S.—**Life of Antonis Rosmini Serbati** (Founder of the Institute of Charity). 2 vols. Demy 8vo.
[Vol. I. now ready, price 12*s.*

MAGNUS, Mrs.—**About the Jews since Bible Times.** From the Babylonian Exile till the English Exodus. Small crown 8vo, 6*s.*

MAIR, R. S., M.D., F.R.C.S.E.—**The Medical Guide for Anglo-Indians.** Being a Compendium of Advice to Europeans in India, relating to the Preservation and Regulation of Health. With a Supplement on the Management of Children in India. Second Edition. Crown 8vo, limp cloth, 3*s.* 6*d.*

MALDEN, Henry Elliot.—**Vienna, 1683.** The History and Consequences of the Defeat of the Turks before Vienna, September 12th, 1683, by John Sobieski, King of Poland, and Charles Leopold, Duke of Lorraine. Crown 8vo, 4*s.* 6*d.*

Many Voices. A volume of Extracts from the Religious Writers of Christendom from the First to the Sixteenth Century. With Biographical Sketches. Crown 8vo, cloth extra, red edges, 6*s.*

MARKHAM, Capt. Albert Hastings, R.N.—**The Great Frozen Sea:** A Personal Narrative of the Voyage of the *Alert* during the Arctic Expedition of 1875–6. With 6 Full-page Illustrations, 2 Maps, and 27 Woodcuts. Sixth and Cheaper Edition. Crown 8vo, 6*s.*

A Polar Reconnaissance: being the Voyage of the *Isbjörn* to Novaya Zemlya in 1879. With 10 Illustrations. Demy 8vo, 16*s.*

Marriage and Maternity; or, Scripture Wives and Mothers. Small crown 8vo, 4*s.* 6*d.*

MARTINEAU, Gertrude.—**Outline Lessons on Morals.** Small crown 8vo, 3*s.* 6*d.*

MAUDSLEY, H., M.D.—**Body and Will.** Being an Essay concerning Will, in its Metaphysical, Physiological, and Pathological Aspects. 8vo, 12*s.*

McGRATH, Terence.—**Pictures from Ireland.** New and Cheaper Edition. Crown 8vo, 2*s.*

MEREDITH, M.A.—**Theotokos, the Example for Woman.** Dedicated, by permission, to Lady Agnes Wood. Revised by the Venerable Archdeacon DENISON. 32mo, limp cloth, 1*s.* 6*d.*

MILLER, Edward.—**The History and Doctrines of Irvingism;** or, the so-called Catholic and Apostolic Church. 2 vols. Large post 8vo, 25*s.*

The Church in Relation to the State. Large crown 8vo, 7*s.* 6*d.*

MINCHIN, J. G.—**Bulgaria since the War:** Notes of a Tour in the Autumn of 1879. Small crown 8vo, 3*s.* 6*d.*

MITFORD, Bertram.—**Through the Zulu Country.** Its Battle-fields and its People. With five Illustrations. Demy 8vo, 14*s.*

MIVART, St. George.—**Nature and Thought:** An Introduction to a Natural Philosophy. Demy 8vo, 10*s.* 6*d.*

MOCKLER, E.—**A Grammar of the Baloochee Language,** as it is spoken in Makran (Ancient Gedrosia), in the Persia-Arabic and Roman characters. Fcap. 8vo, 5*s.*

MOLESWORTH, Rev. W. Nassau, M.A.—**History of the Church of England from 1660.** Large crown 8vo, 7*s.* 6*d.*

MORELL, J. R.—**Euclid Simplified in Method and Language.** Being a Manual of Geometry. Compiled from the most important French Works, approved by the University of Paris and the Minister of Public Instruction. Fcap. 8vo, 2*s.* 6*d.*

MORSE, E. S., Ph.D.—**First Book of Zoology.** With numerous Illustrations. New and Cheaper Edition. Crown 8vo, 2*s.* 6*d.*

MURPHY, John Nicholas.—**The Chair of Peter;** or, the Papacy considered in its Institution, Development, and Organization, and in the Benefits which for over Eighteen Centuries it has conferred on Mankind. Demy 8vo, 18*s.*

NELSON, J. H., M.A.—**A Prospectus of the Scientific Study of the Hindû Law.** Demy 8vo, 9*s.*

NEWMAN, J. H., D.D.—**Characteristics from the Writings of.** Being Selections from his various Works. Arranged with the Author's personal Approval. Sixth Edition. With Portrait. Crown 8vo, 6*s.*

*** A Portrait of Cardinal Newman, mounted for framing, can be had, 2*s.* 6*d.*

NEWMAN, Francis William.—**Essays on Diet.** Small crown 8vo, cloth limp, 2*s.*

New Werther. By LOKI. Small crown 8vo, 2*s.* 6*d.*

NICHOLSON, Edward Byron.—**The Gospel according to the Hebrews.** Its Fragments Translated and Annotated with a Critical Analysis of the External and Internal Evidence relating to it. Demy 8vo, 9*s*. 6*d*.

A New Commentary on the Gospel according to Matthew. Demy 8vo, 12*s*.

NICOLS, Arthur, F.G.S., F.R.G.S.—**Chapters from the Physical History of the Earth:** an Introduction to Geology and Palæontology. With numerous Illustrations. Crown 8vo, 5*s*.

NOPS, Marianne.—**Class Lessons on Euclid.** Part I. containing the First two Books of the Elements. Crown 8vo, 2*s*. 6*d*.

Notes on St. Paul's Epistle to the Galatians. For Readers of the Authorized Version or the Original Greek. Demy 8vo, 2*s*. 6*d*.

Nuces: EXERCISES ON THE SYNTAX OF THE PUBLIC SCHOOL LATIN PRIMER. New Edition in Three Parts. Crown 8vo, each 1*s*.

*** The Three Parts can also be had bound together, 3*s*.

OATES, Frank, F.R.G.S.—**Matabele Land and the Victoria Falls.** A Naturalist's Wanderings in the Interior of South Africa. Edited by C. G. OATES, B.A. With numerous Illustrations and 4 Maps. Demy 8vo, 21*s*.

OGLE, W., M.D., F.R.C.P.—**Aristotle on the Parts of Animals.** Translated, with Introduction and Notes. Royal 8vo, 12*s*. 6*d*.

Oken Lorenz, Life of. By ALEXANDER ECKER. With Explanatory Notes, Selections from Oken's Correspondence, and Portrait of the Professor. From the German by ALFRED TULK. Crown 8vo, 6*s*.

O'MEARA, Kathleen.—**Frederic Ozanam,** Professor of the Sorbonne: His Life and Work. Second Edition. Crown 8vo, 7*s*. 6*d*.

Henri Perreyve and his Counsels to the Sick. Small crown 8vo, 5*s*.

OSBORNE, Rev. W. A.—**The Revised Version of the New Testament.** A Critical Commentary, with Notes upon the Text. Crown 8vo, 5*s*.

OTTLEY, H. Bickersteth.—**The Great Dilemma.** Christ His Own Witness or His Own Accuser. Six Lectures. Second Edition. Crown 8vo, 3*s*. 6*d*.

Our Public Schools—Eton, Harrow, Winchester, Rugby, Westminster, Marlborough, The Charterhouse. Crown 8vo, 6*s*.

OWEN, F. M.—**John Keats:** a Study. Crown 8vo, 6*s*.

OWEN, Rev. Robert, B.D.—**Sanctorale Catholicum;** or, Book of Saints. With Notes, Critical, Exegetical, and Historical. Demy 8vo, 18*s*.

OXENHAM, Rev. F. Nutcombe.—**What is the Truth as to Everlasting Punishment.** Part II. Being an Historical Inquiry into the Witness and Weight of certain Anti-Origenist Councils. Crown 8vo, 2*s.* 6*d.*

OXONIENSES.—**Romanism, Protestantism, Anglicanism.** Being a Layman's View of some questions of the Day. Together with Remarks on Dr. Littledale's "Plain Reasons against joining the Church of Rome." Crown 8vo, 3*s.* 6*d.*

PALMER, the late William.—**Notes of a Visit to Russia in 1840-1841.** Selected and arranged by JOHN H. CARDINAL NEWMAN, with portrait. Crown 8vo, 8*s.* 6*d.*

Parchment Library. Choicely Printed on hand-made paper, limp parchment antique, 6*s.*; vellum, 7*s.* 6*d.* each volume.

English Lyrics.

The Sonnets of John Milton. Edited by MARK PATTISON. With Portrait after Vertue.

Poems by Alfred Tennyson. 2 vols. With minature frontispieces by W. B. Richmond.

French Lyrics. Selected and Annotated by GEORGE SAINTSBURY. With a minature frontispiece designed and etched by H. G. Glindoni.

The Fables of Mr. John Gay. With Memoir by AUSTIN DOBSON, and an etched portrait from an unfinished Oil Sketch by Sir Godfrey Kneller.

Select Letters of Percy Bysshe Shelley. Edited, with an Introduction, by RICHARD GARNETT.

The Christian Year. Thoughts in Verse for the Sundays and Holy Days throughout the Year. With Miniature Portrait of the Rev. J. Keble, after a Drawing by G. Richmond, R.A.

Shakspere's Works. Complete in Twelve Volumes.

Eighteenth Century Essays. Selected and Edited by AUSTIN DOBSON. With a Miniature Frontispiece by R. Caldecott.

Q. Horati Flacci Opera. Edited by F. A. CORNISH, Assistant Master at Eton. With a Frontispiece after a design by L. Alma Tadema, etched by Leopold Lowenstam.

Edgar Allan Poe's Poems. With an Essay on his Poetry by ANDREW LANG, and a Frontispiece by Linley Sambourne.

Shakspere's Sonnets. Edited by EDWARD DOWDEN. With a Frontispiece etched by Leopold Lowenstam, after the Death Mask.

English Odes. Selected by EDMUND W. GOSSE. With Frontispiece on India paper by Hamo Thornycroft, A.R.A.

Of the Imitation of Christ. By THOMAS À KEMPIS. A revised Translation. With Frontispiece on India paper, from a Design by W. B. Richmond.

Parchment Library—*continued.*

Tennyson's The Princess: a Medley. With a Miniature Frontispiece by H. M. Paget, and a Tailpiece in Outline by Gordon Browne.

Poems: Selected from PERCY BYSSHE SHELLEY. Dedicated to Lady Shelley. With a Preface by RICHARD GARNETT and a Miniature Frontispiece.

Tennyson's "In Memoriam." With a Miniature Portrait in *eau-forte* by Le Rat, after a Photograph by the late Mrs. Cameron.

PARSLOE, Joseph.—**Our Railways.** Sketches, Historical and Descriptive. With Practical Information as to Fares and Rates, etc., and a Chapter on Railway Reform. Crown 8vo, 6*s.*

PAUL, C. Kegan.—**Biographical Sketches.** Printed on hand-made paper, bound in buckram. Second Edition. Crown 8vo, 7*s.* 6*d.*

PAUL, Alexander.—**Short Parliaments.** A History of the National Demand for frequent General Elections. Small crown 8vo, 3*s.* 6*d.*

PEARSON, Rev. S.—**Week-day Living.** A Book for Young Men and Women. Second Edition. Crown 8vo, 5*s.*

PENRICE, Maj. J., B.A.—**A Dictionary and Glossary of the Ko-ran.** With Copious Grammatical References and Explanations of the Text. 4to, 21*s.*

PESCHEL, Dr. Oscar.—**The Races of Man and their Geographical Distribution.** Large crown 8vo, 9*s.*

PETERS, F. H.—**The Nicomachean Ethics of Aristotle.** Translated by. Crown 8vo, 6*s.*

PHIPSON, E.—**The Animal Lore of Shakspeare's Time.** Including Quadrupeds, Birds, Reptiles, Fish and Insects. Large post 8vo, 9*s.*

PIDGEON, D.—**An Engineer's Holiday**; or, Notes of a Round Trip from Long. 0° to 0°. New and Cheaper Edition. Large crown 8vo, 7*s.* 6*d.*

PRICE, Prof. Bonamy.—**Currency and Banking.** Crown 8vo, 6*s.*

Chapters on Practical Political Economy. Being the Substance of Lectures delivered before the University of Oxford. New and Cheaper Edition. Large post 8vo, 5*s.*

Pulpit Commentary, The. (Old Testament Series.) Edited by the Rev. J. S. EXELL and the Rev. Canon H. D. M. SPENCE.

Genesis. By the Rev. T. WHITELAW, M.A.; with Homilies by the Very Rev. J. F. MONTGOMERY, D.D., Rev. Prof. R. A. REDFORD, M.A., LL.B., Rev. F. HASTINGS, Rev. W. ROBERTS, M.A. An Introduction to the Study of the Old Testament by the Venerable Archdeacon FARRAR, D.D., F.R.S.; and Introductions to the Pentateuch by the Right Rev. H. COTTERILL, D.D., and Rev. T. WHITELAW, M.A. Seventh Edition. 1 vol., 15*s.*

Pulpit Commentary, The—*continued.*

Exodus. By the Rev. Canon RAWLINSON. With Homilies by Rev. J. ORR, Rev. D. YOUNG, Rev. C. A. GOODHART, Rev. J. URQUHART, and the Rev. H. T. ROBJOHNS. Third Edition. 2 vols., 18*s.*

Leviticus. By the Rev. Prebendary MEYRICK, M.A. With Introductions by the Rev. R. COLLINS, Rev. Professor A. CAVE, and Homilies by Rev. Prof. REDFORD, LL.B., Rev. J. A. MACDONALD, Rev. W. CLARKSON, Rev. S. R. ALDRIDGE, LL.B., and Rev. McCHEYNE EDGAR. Fourth Edition. 15*s.*

Numbers. By the Rev. R. WINTERBOTHAM, LL.B.; with Homilies by the Rev. Professor W. BINNIE, D.D., Rev. E. S. PROUT, M.A., Rev. D. YOUNG, Rev. J. WAITE, and an Introduction by the Rev. THOMAS WHITELAW, M.A. Fourth Edition. 15*s.*

Deuteronomy. By the Rev. W. L. ALEXANDER, D.D. With Homilies by Rev. C. CLEMANCE, D.D., Rev. J. ORR, B.D., Rev. R. M. EDGAR, M.A., Rev. D. DAVIES, M.A. Third edition. 15*s.*

Joshua. By Rev. J. J. LIAS, M.A.; with Homilies by Rev. S. R. ALDRIDGE, LL.B., Rev. R. GLOVER, REV. E. DE PRESSENSÉ, D.D., Rev. J. WAITE, B.A., Rev. F. W. ADENEY, M.A.; and an Introduction by the Rev. A. PLUMMER, M.A. Fifth Edition. 12*s.* 6*d.*

Judges and Ruth. By the Bishop of Bath and Wells, and Rev. J. MORRISON, D.D.; with Homilies by Rev. A. F. MUIR, M.A., Rev. W. F. ADENEY, M.A., Rev. W. M. STATHAM, and Rev. Professor J. THOMSON, M.A. Fourth Edition. 10*s.* 6*d.*

1 Samuel. By the Very Rev. R. P. SMITH, D.D.; with Homilies by Rev. DONALD FRASER, D.D., Rev. Prof. CHAPMAN, and Rev. B. DALE. Sixth Edition. 15*s.*

1 Kings. By the Rev. JOSEPH HAMMOND, LL.B. With Homilies by the Rev. E. DE PRESSENSÉ, D.D., Rev. J. WAITE, B.A., Rev. A. ROWLAND, LL.B., Rev. J. A. MACDONALD, and Rev. J. URQUHART. Fourth Edition. 15*s.*

Ezra, Nehemiah, and Esther. By Rev. Canon G. RAWLINSON, M.A.; with Homilies by Rev. Prof. J. R. THOMSON, M.A., Rev. Prof. R. A. REDFORD, LL.B., M.A., Rev. W. S. LEWIS, M.A., Rev. J. A. MACDONALD, Rev. A. MACKENNAL, B.A., Rev. W. CLARKSON, B.A., Rev. F. HASTINGS, Rev. W. DINWIDDIE, LL.B., Rev. Prof. ROWLANDS, B.A., Rev. G. WOOD, B.A., Rev. Prof. P. C. BARKER, LL.B., M.A., and the Rev. J. S. EXELL. Sixth Edition. 1 vol., 12*s.* 6*d.*

Jeremiah. By the Rev. J. K. CHEYNE, M.A.; with Homilies by the Rev. W. F. ADENEY, M.A., Rev. A. F. MUIR, M.A., Rev. S. CONWAY, B.A., Rev. J. WAITE, B.A., and Rev. D. YOUNG, B.A. Vol. I., 15s.

Pulpit Commentary, The. (New Testament Series.)
St. Mark. By Very Rev. E. BICKERSTETH, D.D., Dean of Lichfield; with Homilies by Rev. Prof. THOMSON, M.A., Rev. Prof. GIVEN, M.A., Rev. Prof. JOHNSON, M.A., Rev. A. ROWLAND, B.A., LL.B., Rev. A. MUIR, and Rev. R. GREEN. 2 vols. Third Edition. 21*s.*

PUSEY, Dr.—**Sermons for the Church's Seasons from Advent to Trinity.** Selected from the Published Sermons of the late EDWARD BOUVERIE PUSEY, D.D. Crown 8vo, 5*s.*

QUILTER, Harry.—**"The Academy," 1872-1882.**

RADCLIFFE, Frank R. Y.—**The New Politicus.** Small crown 8vo, 2*s.* 6*d.*

Realities of the Future Life. Small crown 8vo, 1*s.* 6*d.*

RENDELL, J. M.—**Concise Handbook of the Island of Madeira.** With Plan of Funchal and Map of the Island. Fcap. 8vo, 1*s.* 6*d.*

REYNOLDS, Rev. J. W.—**The Supernatural in Nature.** A Verification by Free Use of Science. Third Edition, Revised and Enlarged. Demy 8vo, 14*s.*

The Mystery of Miracles. Third and Enlarged Edition. Crown 8vo, 6*s.*

RIBOT, Prof. Th.—**Heredity:** A Psychological Study on its Phenomena, its Laws, its Causes, and its Consequences. Large crown 8vo, 9*s.*

ROBERTSON, The late Rev. F. W., M.A.—**Life and Letters of.** Edited by the Rev. STOPFORD BROOKE, M.A.

I. Two vols., uniform with the Sermons. With Steel Portrait. Crown 8vo, 7*s.* 6*d.*

II. Library Edition, in Demy 8vo, with Portrait. 12*s.*

III. A Popular Edition, in 1 vol. Crown 8vo, 6*s.*

Sermons. Four Series. Small crown 8vo, 3*s.* 6*d.* each.

The Human Race, and other Sermons. Preached at Cheltenham, Oxford, and Brighton. New and Cheaper Edition. Crown 8vo, 3*s.* 6*d.*

Notes on Genesis. New and Cheaper Edition. Crown 8vo, 3*s.* 6*d.*

Expository Lectures on St. Paul's Epistles to the Corinthians. A New Edition. Small crown 8vo, 5*s.*

Lectures and Addresses, with other Literary Remains. A New Edition. Crown 8vo, 5*s.*

An Analysis of Mr. Tennyson's "In Memoriam." (Dedicated by Permission to the Poet-Laureate.) Fcap. 8vo, 2*s.*

The Education of the Human Race. Translated from the German of GOTTHOLD EPHRAIM LESSING. Fcap. 8vo, 2*s.* 6*d.*

The above Works can also be had, bound in half morocco.

*** A Portrait of the late Rev. F. W. Robertson, mounted for framing, can be had, 2*s.* 6*d.*

Rosmini Serbati (Life of). By G. STUART MACWALTER. 2 vols. 8vo. [Vol. I. now ready, 12*s*.

Rosmini's Origin of Ideas. Translated from the Fifth Italian Edition of the Nuovo Saggio *Sull' origine delle idee.* 3 vols. Demy 8vo, cloth. [Vols. I. and II. now ready, 16*s*. each.

Rosmini's Philosophical System. Translated, with a Sketch of the Author's Life, Bibliography, Introduction, and Notes by THOMAS DAVIDSON. Demy 8vo, 16*s*.

RULE, Martin, M.A.—**The Life and Times of St. Anselm, Archbishop of Canterbury and Primate of the Britains.** 2 vols. Demy 8vo, 21*s*.

SALVATOR, Archduke Ludwig.—**Levkosia, the Capital of Cyprus.** Crown 4to, 10*s*. 6*d*.

SAMUEL, Sydney M.—**Jewish Life in the East.** Small crown 8vo, 3*s*. 6*d*.

SAYCE, Rev. Archibald Henry.—**Introduction to the Science of Language.** 2 vols. Second Edition. Large post 8vo, 25*s*.

Scientific Layman. The New Truth and the Old Faith: are they Incompatible? Demy 8vo, 10*s*. 6*d*.

SCOONES, W. Baptiste.—**Four Centuries of English Letters:** A Selection of 350 Letters by 150 Writers, from the Period of the Paston Letters to the Present Time. Third Edition. Large crown 8vo, 6*s*.

SHILLITO, Rev. Joseph.—**Womanhood:** its Duties, Temptations, and Privileges. A Book for Young Women. Third Edition. Crown 8vo, 3*s*. 6*d*.

SHIPLEY, Rev. Orby, M.A.—**Principles of the Faith in Relation to Sin.** Topics for Thought in Times of Retreat. Eleven Addresses delivered during a Retreat of Three Days to Persons living in the World. Demy 8vo, 12*s*.

Sister Augustine, Superior of the Sisters of Charity at the St. Johannis Hospital at Bonn. Authorised Translation by HANS THARAU, from the German "Memorials of AMALIE VON LASAULX." Cheap Edition. Large crown 8vo, 4*s*. 6*d*.

SMITH, Edward, M.D., LL.B., F.R.S.—**Tubercular Consumption in its Early and Remediable Stages.** Second Edition. Crown 8vo, 6*s*.

SPEDDING, James.—**Reviews and Discussions, Literary, Political, and Historical not relating to Bacon.** Demy 8vo, 12*s*. 6*d*.

Evenings with a Reviewer; or, Bacon and Macaulay. With a Prefatory Notice by G. S. VENABLES, Q.C. 2 vols. Demy 8vo, 18*s*.

STAPFER, Paul.—**Shakspeare and Classical Antiquity:** Greek and Latin Antiquity as presented in Shakspeare's Plays. Translated by EMILY J. CAREY. Large post 8vo, 12*s.*

STEVENSON, Rev. W. F.—**Hymns for the Church and Home.** Selected and Edited by the Rev. W. FLEMING STEVENSON.

The Hymn Book consists of Three Parts:—I. For Public Worship.—II. For Family and Private Worship.—III. For Children.

*** Published in various forms and prices, the latter ranging from 8*d.* to 6*s.*

Lists and full particulars will be furnished on application to the Publishers.

STEVENSON, Robert Louis.—**Travels with a Donkey in the Cevennes.** With Frontispiece by Walter Crane. Small crown 8vo, 2*s.* 6*d.*

An Inland Voyage. With Frontispiece by Walter Crane. Small Crown 8vo, 2*s.* 6*d.*

Virginibus Puerisque, and other Papers. Crown 8vo, 6*s.*

Stray Papers on Education, and Scenes from School Life. By B. H. Small crown 8vo, 3*s.* 6*d.*

STRECKER-WISLICENUS.—**Organic Chemistry.** Translated and Edited, with Extensive Additions, by W. R. HODGKINSON, Ph.D., and A. J. GREENAWAY, F.I.C. Demy 8vo, 21*s.*

SULLY, James, M.A.—**Pessimism:** a History and a Criticism. Second Edition. Demy 8vo, 14*s.*

SWEDENBORG, Eman.—**De Cultu et Amore Dei ubi Agitur de Telluris ortu, Paradiso et Vivario, tum de Primogeniti Seu Adami Nativitate Infantia, et Amore.** Crown 8vo, 5*s.*

SYME, David.—**Representative Government in England.** Its Faults and Failures. Second Edition. Large crown 8vo, 6*s.*

TAYLOR, Rev. Isaac.—**The Alphabet.** An Account of the Origin and Development of Letters. With numerous Tables and Facsimiles. 2 vols. Demy 8vo, 36*s.*

Thirty Thousand Thoughts. Edited by the Rev. CANON SPENCE, Rev. J. S. EXELL, Rev. CHARLES NEIL, and Rev. JACOB STEPHENSON. 6 vols. Super royal 8vo.

[Vol. I. now ready, 16*s.*

THOM, J. Hamilton.—**Laws of Life after the Mind of Christ.** Second Edition. Crown 8vo, 7*s.* 6*d.*

THOMSON, J. Turnbull.—**Social Problems; or, An Inquiry into the Laws of Influence.** With Diagrams. Demy 8vo, 10*s.* 6*d.*

TIDMAN, Paul F.—**Gold and Silver Money.** Part I.—A Plain Statement. Part II.—Objections Answered. Third Edition. Crown 8vo, 1*s.*

TIPPLE, Rev. S. A.—**Sunday Mornings at Norwood.** Prayers and Sermons. Crown 8vo, 6*s.*

TODHUNTER, Dr. J.—**A Study of Shelley.** Crown 8vo, 7*s.*

TREMENHEERE, Hugh Seymour, C.B.—**A Manual of the Principles of Government,** as set forth by the Authorities of Ancient and Modern Times. New and Enlarged Edition. Crown 8vo, 5*s.*

TUKE, Daniel Hack, M.D., F.R.C.P.—**Chapters in the History of the Insane in the British Isles.** With 4 Illustrations. Large crown 8vo, 12*s.*

TWINING, Louisa.—**Workhouse Visiting and Management during Twenty-Five Years.** Small crown 8vo, 3*s.* 6*d.*

TYLER, J.—**The Mystery of Being: or, What Do We Know?** Small crown 8vo, 3*s.* 6*d.*

UPTON, Major R. D.—**Gleanings from the Desert of Arabia.** Large post 8vo, 10*s.* 6*d.*

VACUUS, Viator.—**Flying South.** Recollections of France and its Littoral. Small crown 8vo, 3*s.* 6*d.*

VAUGHAN, H. Halford.—**New Readings and Renderings of Shakespeare's Tragedies.** 2 vols. Demy 8vo, 25*s.*

VILLARI, Professor.—**Niccolò Machiavelli and his Times.** Translated by Linda Villari. 4 vols. Large post 8vo, 48*s.*

VILLIERS, The Right Hon. C. P.—**Free Trade Speeches of.** With Political Memoir. Edited by a Member of the Cobden Club. 2 vols. With Portrait. Demy 8vo, 25*s.*

VOGT, Lieut.-Col. Hermann.—**The Egyptian War of 1882.** A translation. With Map and Plans. Large crown 8vo, 6*s.*

VOLCKXSOM, E. W. V.—**Catechism of Elementary Modern Chemistry.** Small crown 8vo, 3*s.*

VYNER, Lady Mary.—**Every Day a Portion.** Adapted from the Bible and the Prayer Book, for the Private Devotion of those living in Widowhood. Collected and Edited by Lady Mary Vyner, Square crown 8vo, 5*s.*

WALDSTEIN, Charles, Ph.D.—**The Balance of Emotion and Intellect;** an Introductory Essay to the Study of Philosophy. Crown 8vo, 6*s.*

WALLER, Rev. C. B.—**The Apocalypse,** reviewed under the Light of the Doctrine of the Unfolding Ages, and the Restitution of All Things. Demy 8vo, 12*s.*

WALPOLE, Chas. George.—**History of Ireland from the Earliest Times to the Union with Great Britain.** With 5 Maps and Appendices. Crown 8vo, 10*s.* 6*d.*

WALSHE, Walter Hayle, M.D.—**Dramatic Singing Physiologically Estimated.** Crown 8vo, 3*s.* 6*d.*

WEDMORE, Frederick.—**The Masters of Genre Painting.** With Sixteen Illustrations. Crown 8vo, 7*s.* 6*d.*

WHEWELL, William, D.D.—**His Life and Selections from his Correspondence.** By Mrs. STAIR DOUGLAS. With a Portrait from a Painting by Samuel Laurence. Demy 8vo, 21*s.*

WHITNEY, Prof. William Dwight.—**Essentials of English Grammar,** for the Use of Schools. Crown 8vo, 3*s.* 6*d.*

WILLIAMS, Rowland, D.D.—**Psalms, Litanies, Counsels, and Collects for Devout Persons.** Edited by his Widow. New and Popular Edition. Crown 8vo, 3*s.* 6*d.*

Stray Thoughts Collected from the Writings of the late Rowland Williams, D.D. Edited by his Widow. Crown 8vo, 3*s.* 6*d.*

WILLIS, R., M.A.—**William Harvey.** A History of the Discovery of the Circulation of the Blood: with a Portrait of Harvey after Faithorne. Demy 8vo, 14*s.*

WILSON, Sir Erasmus.—**Egypt of the Past.** With Chromo-lithograph and numerous Illustrations in the text. Second Edition, Revised. Crown 8vo, 12*s.*

The Recent Archaic Discovery of Egyptian Mummies at Thebes. A Lecture. Crown 8vo, 1*s.* 6*d.*

WILSON, Lieut.-Col. C. T.—**The Duke of Berwick, Marshall of France, 1702-1734.** Demy 8vo, 15*s.*

WOLTMANN, Dr. Alfred, and WOERMANN, Dr. Karl.—**History of Painting.** Edited by SIDNEY COLVIN. Vol. I. Painting in Antiquity and the Middle Ages. With numerous Illustrations. Medium 8vo, 28*s.*; bevelled boards, gilt leaves, 30*s.*

Word was Made Flesh. Short Family Readings on the Epistles for each Sunday of the Christian Year. Demy 8vo, 10*s.* 6*d.*

WREN, Sir Christopher.—**His Family and His Times.** With Original Letters, and a Discourse on Architecture hitherto unpublished. By LUCY PHILLIMORE. With Portrait. Demy 8vo, 14*s.*

YOUMANS, Eliza A.—**First Book of Botany.** Designed to Cultivate the Observing Powers of Children. With 300 Engravings. New and Cheaper Edition. Crown 8vo, 2*s.* 6*d.*

YOUMANS, Edward L., M.D.—**A Class Book of Chemistry,** on the Basis of the New System. With 200 Illustrations. Crown 8vo, 5*s.*

THE INTERNATIONAL SCIENTIFIC SERIES.

I. **Forms of Water**: a Familiar Exposition of the Origin and Phenomena of Glaciers. By J. Tyndall, LL.D., F.R.S. With 25 Illustrations. Eighth Edition. Crown 8vo, 5*s*.

II. **Physics and Politics**; or, Thoughts on the Application of the Principles of "Natural Selection" and "Inheritance" to Political Society. By Walter Bagehot. Sixth Edition. Crown 8vo, 4*s*.

III. **Foods.** By Edward Smith, M.D., LL.B., F.R.S. With numerous Illustrations. Eighth Edition. Crown 8vo, 5*s*.

IV. **Mind and Body**: the Theories of their Relation. By Alexander Bain, LL.D. With Four Illustrations. Seventh Edition. Crown 8vo, 4*s*.

V. **The Study of Sociology.** By Herbert Spencer. Eleventh Edition. Crown 8vo, 5*s*.

VI. **On the Conservation of Energy.** By Balfour Stewart, M.A., LL.D., F.R.S. With 14 Illustrations. Sixth Edition. Crown 8vo, 5*s*.

VII. **Animal Locomotion**; or Walking, Swimming, and Flying. By J. B. Pettigrew, M.D., F.R.S., etc. With 130 Illustrations. Third Edition. Crown 8vo, 5*s*.

VIII. **Responsibility in Mental Disease.** By Henry Maudsley, M.D. Fourth Edition. Crown 8vo, 5*s*.

IX. **The New Chemistry.** By Professor J. P. Cooke. With 31 Illustrations. Seventh Edition. Crown 8vo, 5*s*.

X. **The Science of Law.** By Professor Sheldon Amos. Fifth Edition. Crown 8vo, 5*s*.

XI. **Animal Mechanism**: a Treatise on Terrestrial and Aerial Locomotion. By Professor E. J. Marey. With 117 Illustrations. Third Edition. Crown 8vo, 5*s*.

XII. **The Doctrine of Descent and Darwinism.** By Professor Oscar Schmidt. With 26 Illustrations. Fifth Edition. Crown 8vo, 5*s*.

XIII. **The History of the Conflict between Religion and Science.** By J. W. Draper, M.D., LL.D. Seventeenth Edition. Crown 8vo, 5*s*.

XIV. **Fungi**: their Nature, Influences, Uses, etc. By M. C. Cooke, M.D., LL.D. Edited by the Rev. M. J. Berkeley, M.A., F.L.S. With numerous Illustrations. Third Edition. Crown 8vo, 5*s*.

XV. **The Chemical Effects of Light and Photography.** By Dr. Hermann Vogel. Translation thoroughly Revised. With 100 Illustrations. Fourth Edition. Crown 8vo, 5*s*.

XVI. **The Life and Growth of Language.** By Professor William Dwight Whitney. Fourth Edition. Crown 8vo, 5*s.*

XVII. **Money and the Mechanism of Exchange.** By W. Stanley Jevons, M.A., F.R.S. Sixth Edition. Crown 8vo, 5*s.*

XVIII. **The Nature of Light.** With a General Account of Physical Optics. By Dr. Eugene Lommel. With 188 Illustrations and a Table of Spectra in Chromo-lithography. Third Edition. Crown 8vo, 5*s.*

XIX. **Animal Parasites and Messmates.** By Monsieur Van Beneden. With 83 Illustrations. Third Edition. Crown 8vo, 5*s.*

XX. **Fermentation.** By Professor Schützenberger. With 28 Illustrations. Third Edition. Crown 8vo, 5*s.*

XXI. **The Five Senses of Man.** By Professor Bernstein. With 91 Illustrations. Fourth Edition. Crown 8vo, 5*s.*

XXII. **The Theory of Sound in its Relation to Music.** By Professor Pietro Blaserna. With numerous Illustrations. Third Edition. Crown 8vo, 5*s.*

XXIII. **Studies in Spectrum Analysis.** By J. Norman Lockyer, F.R.S. With six photographic Illustrations of Spectra, and numerous engravings on Wood. Third Edition. Crown 8vo, 6*s.* 6*d.*

XXIV. **A History of the Growth of the Steam Engine.** By Professor R. H. Thurston. With numerous Illustrations. Third Edition. Crown 8vo, 6*s.* 6*d.*

XXV. **Education as a Science.** By Alexander Bain, LL.D. Fourth Edition. Crown 8vo, 5*s.*

XXVI. **The Human Species.** By Professor A. de Quatrefages. Third Edition. Crown 8vo, 5*s.*

XXVII. **Modern Chromatics.** With Applications to Art and Industry. By Ogden N. Rood. With 130 original Illustrations. Second Edition. Crown 8vo, 5*s.*

XXVIII. **The Crayfish: an Introduction to the Study of Zoology.** By Professor T. H. Huxley. With 82 Illustrations. Third Edition. Crown 8vo, 5*s.*

XXIX. **The Brain as an Organ of Mind.** By H. Charlton Bastian, M.D. With numerous Illustrations. Third Edition. Crown 8vo, 5*s.*

XXX. **The Atomic Theory.** By Prof. Wurtz. Translated by G. Cleminshaw, F.C.S. Third Edition. Crown 8vo, 5*s.*

XXXI. **The Natural Conditions of Existence as they affect Animal Life.** By Karl Semper. With 2 Maps and 106 Woodcuts. Third Edition. Crown 8vo, 5*s.*

XXXII. **General Physiology of Muscles and Nerves.** By Prof. J. Rosenthal. Third Edition. With Illustrations. Crown 8vo, 5*s*.

XXXIII. **Sight:** an Exposition of the Principles of Monocular and Binocular Vision. By Joseph le Conte, LL.D. Second Edition. With 132 Illustrations. Crown 8vo, 5*s*.

XXXIV. **Illusions:** a Psychological Study. By James Sully. Second Edition. Crown 8vo, 5*s*.

XXXV. **Volcanoes: what they are and what they teach.** By Professor J. W. Judd, F.R.S. With 92 Illustrations on Wood. Second Edition. Crown 8vo, 5*s*.

XXXVI. **Suicide:** an Essay in Comparative Moral Statistics. By Prof. E. Morselli. Second Edition. With Diagrams. Crown 8vo, 5*s*.

XXXVII. **The Brain and its Functions.** By J. Luys. With Illustrations. Second Edition. Crown 8vo, 5*s*.

XXXVIII. **Myth and Science:** an Essay. By Tito Vignoli. Crown 8vo, 5*s*.

XXXIX. **The Sun.** By Professor Young. With Illustrations. Second Edition. Crown 8vo, 5*s*.

XL. **Ants, Bees, and Wasps:** a Record of Observations on the Habits of the Social Hymenoptera. By Sir John Lubbock, Bart., M.P. With 5 Chromo-lithographic Illustrations. Sixth Edition. Crown 8vo, 5*s*.

XLI. **Animal Intelligence.** By G. J. Romanes, LL.D., F.R.S. Third Edition. Crown 8vo, 5*s*.

XLII. **The Concepts and Theories of Modern Physics.** By J. B. Stallo. Second Edition. Crown 8vo, 5*s*.

XLIII. **Diseases of the Memory;** An Essay in the Positive Psychology. By Prof. Th. Ribot. Second Edition. Crown 8vo, 5*s*.

XLIV. **Man before Metals.** By N. Joly, with 148 Illustrations. Third Edition. Crown 8vo, 5*s*.

XLV. **The Science of Politics.** By Prof. Sheldon Amos. Second Edition. Crown 8vo, 5*s*.

XLVI. **Elementary Meteorology.** By Robert H. Scott. Second Edition. With Numerous Illustrations. Crown 8vo, 5*s*.

XLVII. **The Organs of Speech and their Application in the Formation of Articulate Sounds.** By George Hermann Von Meyer. With 47 Woodcuts. Crown 8vo, 5*s*.

XLVIII. **Fallacies.** A View of Logic from the Practical Side. By Alfred Sidgwick.

MILITARY WORKS.

BARRINGTON, Capt. J. T.—**England on the Defensive**; or, the Problem of Invasion Critically Examined. Large crown 8vo, with Map, 7*s*. 6*d*.

BRACKENBURY, Col. C. B., R.A., C.B.—**Military Handbooks for Regimental Officers.**

I. **Military Sketching and Reconnaissance.** By Col. F. J. Hutchison, and Major H. G. MacGregor. Fourth Edition. With 15 Plates. Small 8vo, 6*s*.

II. **The Elements of Modern Tactics Practically applied to English Formations.** By Lieut.-Col. Wilkinson Shaw. Fourth Edition. With 25 Plates and Maps. Small crown 8vo, 9*s*.

III. **Field Artillery.** Its Equipment, Organization and Tactics. By Major Sisson C. Pratt, R.A. With 12 Plates. Second Edition. Small crown 8vo, 6*s*.

IV. **The Elements of Military Administration.** First Part: Permanent System of Administration. By Major J. W. Buxton. Small crown 8vo. 7*s*. 6*d*.

V. **Military Law:** Its Procedure and Practice. By Major Sisson C. Pratt, R.A. Small crown 8vo.

BROOKE, Major, C. K.—**A System of Field Training.** Small crown 8vo, cloth limp, 2*s*.

CLERY, C., Lieut.-Col.—**Minor Tactics.** With 26 Maps and Plans. Sixth and Cheaper Edition, Revised. Crown 8vo, 9*s*.

COLVILE, Lieut.-Col. C. F.—**Military Tribunals.** Sewed, 2*s*. 6*d*.

HARRISON, Lieut.-Col. R.—**The Officer's Memorandum Book for Peace and War.** Third Edition. Oblong 32mo, roan, with pencil, 3*s*. 6*d*.

Notes on Cavalry Tactics, Organisation, etc. By a Cavalry Officer. With Diagrams. Demy 8vo, 12*s*.

PARR, Capt. H. Hallam, C.M.G.—**The Dress, Horses, and Equipment of Infantry and Staff Officers.** Crown 8vo, 1*s*.

SCHAW, Col. H.—**The Defence and Attack of Positions and Localities.** Second Edition, Revised and Corrected. Crown 8vo, 3*s*. 6*d*.

SHADWELL, Maj.-Gen., C.B.—**Mountain Warfare.** Illustrated by the Campaign of 1799 in Switzerland. Being a Translation of the Swiss Narrative compiled from the Works of the Archduke Charles, Jomini, and others. Also of Notes by General H. Dufour on the Campaign of the Valtelline in 1635. With Appendix, Maps, and Introductory Remarks. Demy 8vo, 16*s*.

STUBBS, Lieut.-Col. F. W.—**The Regiment of Bengal Artillery.** The History of its Organisation, Equipment, and War Services. Compiled from Published Works, Official Records, and various Private Sources. With numerous Maps and Illustrations. 2 vols. Demy 8vo, 32*s.*

POETRY.

ADAM OF ST. VICTOR.—**The Liturgical Poetry of Adam of St. Victor.** From the text of GAUTIER. With Translations into English in the Original Metres, and Short Explanatory Notes, by DIGBY S. WRANGHAM, M.A. 3 vols. Crown 8vo, printed on hand-made paper, boards, 21*s.*

AUCHMUTY, A. C.—**Poems of English Heroism:** From Brunanburh to Lucknow; from Athelstan to Albert. Small crown 8vo, 1*s.* 6*d.*

AVIA.—**The Odyssey of Homer.** Done into English Verse by. Fcap. 4to, 15*s.*

BANKS, Mrs. G. L.—**Ripples and Breakers:** Poems. Square 8vo, 5*s.*

BARNES, William.—**Poems of Rural Life, in the Dorset Dialect.** New Edition, complete in one vol. Crown 8vo, 8*s.* 6*d.*

BAYNES, Rev. Canon H. R.—**Home Songs for Quiet Hours.** Fourth and Cheaper Edition. Fcap. 8vo, cloth, 2*s.* 6*d.*

*** This may also be had handsomely bound in morocco with gilt edges.

BENNETT, C. Fletcher.—**Life Thoughts.** A New Volume of Poems. With Frontispiece. Small crown 8vo.

BEVINGTON, L. S.—**Key Notes.** Small crown 8vo, 5*s.*

BILLSON, C. J.—**The Acharnians of Aristophanes.** Crown 8vo, 3*s.* 6*d.*

BOWEN, H. C., M.A.—**Simple English Poems.** English Literature for Junior Classes. In Four Parts. Parts I., II., and III., 6*d.* each, and Part IV., 1*s.*

BRYANT, W. C.—**Poems.** Red-line Edition. With 24 Illustrations and Portrait of the Author. Crown 8vo, extra, 7*s.* 6*d.*

A Cheap Edition, with Frontispiece. Small crown 8vo, 3*s.* 6*d.*

BYRNNE, E. Fairfax.—**Milicent:** a Poem. Small crown 8vo, 6*s.*

Calderon's Dramas: the Wonder-Working Magician—Life is a Dream—the Purgatory of St. Patrick. Translated by DENIS FLORENCE MACCARTHY. Post 8vo, 10*s.*

Castilian Brothers (The), Chateaubriant, Waldemar: Three Tragedies; and **The Rose of Sicily**: a Drama. By the Author of "Ginevra," &c. Crown 8vo, 6*s*.

Chronicles of Christopher Columbus. A Poem in 12 Cantos. By M. D. C. Crown 8vo, 7*s*. 6*d*.

CLARKE, Mary Cowden.—**Honey from the Weed.** Verses. Crown 8vo, 7*s*.

COLOMB, Colonel.—**The Cardinal Archbishop**: a Spanish Legend. In 29 Cancions. Small crown 8vo, 5*s*.

CONWAY, Hugh.—**A Life's Idylls.** Small crown 8vo, 3*s*. 6*d*.

COPPÉE, Francois.—**L'Exilée.** Done into English Verse, with the sanction of the Author, by I. O. L. Crown 8vo, vellum, 5*s*.

COXHEAD, Ethel.—**Birds and Babies.** Imp. 16mo. With 33 Illustrations. Gilt, 2*s*. 6*d*.

David Rizzio, Bothwell, and the Witch Lady. Three Tragedies by the author of "Ginevra," etc. Crown 8vo, 6*s*.

DAVIE, G. S., M.D.—**The Garden of Fragrance.** Being a complete translation of the Bostán of Sádi from the original Persian into English Verse. Crown 8vo, 7*s*. 6*d*.

DAVIES, T. Hart.—**Catullus.** Translated into English Verse. Crown 8vo, 6*s*.

DE VERE, Aubrey.—**The Foray of Queen Meave,** and other Legends of Ireland's Heroic Age. Small crown 8vo, 5*s*.

Legends of the Saxon Saints. Small crown 8vo, 6*s*.

DILLON, Arthur.—**River Songs and other Poems.** With 13 autotype Illustrations from designs by Margery May. Fcap. 4to, cloth extra, gilt leaves, 10*s*. 6*d*.

DOBELL, Mrs. Horace.—**Ethelstone, Eveline,** and other Poems. Crown 8vo, 6*s*.

DOBSON, Austin.—**Old World Idylls** and other Poems. 18mo, cloth extra, gilt tops, 6*s*.

DOMET, Alfred.—**Ranolf and Amohia.** A Dream of Two Lives. New Edition, Revised. 2 vols. Crown 8vo, 12*s*.

Dorothy: a Country Story in Elegiac Verse. With Preface. Demy 8vo, 5*s*.

DOWDEN, Edward, LL.D.—**Shakspere's Sonnets.** With Introduction. Large post 8vo, 7*s*. 6*d*.

DOWNTON, Rev. H., M.A.—**Hymns and Verses.** Original and Translated. Small crown 8vo, 3*s*. 6*d*.

DUTT, Toru.—**A Sheaf Gleaned in French Fields.** New Edition. Demy 8vo, 10*s*. 6*d*.

EDMONDS, E. W.—**Hesperas.** Rhythm and Rhyme. Crown 8vo, 4*s*.

ELDRYTH, Maud.—**Margaret, and other Poems.** Small crown 8vo, 3*s*. 6*d*.

ELLIOTT, Ebenezer, The Corn Law Rhymer.—**Poems.** Edited by his son, the Rev. EDWIN ELLIOTT, of St. John's, Antigua. 2 vols. Crown 8vo, 18*s*.

English Odes. Selected, with a Critical Introduction by EDMUND W. GOSSE, and a miniature frontispiece by Hamo Thornycroft, A.R.A. Elzevir 8vo, limp parchment antique, 6*s*.; vellum, 7*s*. 6*d*.

EVANS, Anne.—**Poems and Music.** With Memorial Preface by ANN THACKERAY RITCHIE. Large crown 8vo, 7*s*.

GOSSE, Edmund W.—**New Poems.** Crown 8vo, 7*s*. 6*d*.

GRAHAM, William. **Two Fancies and other Poems.** Crown 8vo, 5*s*.

GRINDROD, Charles. **Plays from English History.** Crown 8vo, 7*s*. 6*d*.

GURNEY, Rev. Alfred.—**The Vision of the Eucharist, and other Poems.** Crown 8vo, 5*s*.

HELLON, H. G.—**Daphnis: a Pastoral Poem.** Small crown 8vo, 3*s*. 6*d*.

Herman Waldgrave: a Life's Drama. By the Author of "Ginevra," etc. Crown 8vo, 6*s*.

HICKEY, E. H.—**A Sculptor, and other Poems.** Small crown 8vo, 5*s*.

Horati Opera. Edited by F. A. CORNISH, Assistant Master at Eton. With a Frontispiece after a design by L. Alma Tadema, etched by Leopold Lowenstam. Parchment Library Edition, 6*s*.; vellum, 7*s*. 6*d*.

INGHAM, Sarson, C. J.—**Cædmon's Vision, and other Poems.** Small crown 8vo, 5*s*.

JENKINS, Rev. Canon.—**Alfonso Petrucci, Cardinal and Conspirator: an Historical Tragedy in Five Acts.** Small crown 8vo, 3*s*. 6*d*.

KING, Edward.—**Echoes from the Orient.** With Miscellaneous Poems. Small crown 8vo, 3*s*. 6*d*.

KING, Mrs. Hamilton.—**The Disciples.** Fifth Edition, with Portrait and Notes. Crown 8vo, 5*s*.

A Book of Dreams. Crown 8vo, 5*s*.

LANG, A.—**XXXII Ballades in Blue China.** Elzevir 8vo, parchment, 5*s*.

LAWSON, Right Hon. Mr. Justice.—**Hymni Usitati Latine Redditi:** with other Verses. Small 8vo, parchment, 5*s.*

LEIGH, Arran and Isla.—**Bellerophon.** Small crown 8vo, 5*s.*

LEIGHTON, Robert.—**Records,** and other Poems. With Portrait. Small crown 8vo, 7*s.* 6*d.*

Lessings Nathan the Wise. Translated by EUSTACE K. CORBETT. Crown 8vo, 6*s.*

Living English Poets MDCCCLXXXII. With Frontispiece by Walter Crane. Second Edition. Large crown 8vo. Printed on hand-made paper. Parchment, 12*s.*, vellum, 15*s.*

LOCKER, F.—**London Lyrics.** A New and Cheaper Edition. Small crown 8vo, 2*s.* 6*d.*

Love in Idleness. A Volume of Poems. With an etching by W. B. Scott. Small crown 8vo, 5*s.*

Love Sonnets of Proteus. With Frontispiece by the Author. Elzevir 8vo, 5*s.*

LOWNDES, Henry.—**Poems and Translations.** Crown 8vo, 6*s.*

LUMSDEN, Lieut.-Col. H. W.—**Beowulf:** an Old English Poem. Translated into Modern Rhymes. Second Edition. Small crown 8vo, 5*s.*

Lyre and Star. Poems by the Author of "Ginevra," etc. Crown 8vo, 5*s.*

MACLEAN, Charles Donald.—**Latin and Greek Verse Translations.** Small crown 8vo, 2*s.*

MAGNUSSON, Eirikr, M.A., and PALMER, E. H., M.A.—**Johan Ludvig Runeberg's Lyrical Songs, Idylls, and Epigrams.** Fcap. 8vo, 5*s.*

M.D.C.—**Chronicles of Christopher Columbus.** A Poem in Twelve Cantos. Crown 8vo, 7*s.* 6*d.*

MEREDITH, Owen, The Earl of Lytton.—**Lucile.** New Edition. With 32 Illustrations. 16mo, 3*s.* 6*d.* Cloth extra, gilt edges, 4*s.* 6*d.*

MIDDLETON, The Lady.—**Ballads.** Square 16mo, 3*s.* 6*d.*

MORICE, Rev. F. D., M.A.—**The Olympian and Pythian Odes of Pindar.** A New Translation in English Verse. Crown 8vo, 7*s.* 6*d.*

MORRIS, Lewis.—**Poetical Works of.** New and Cheaper Editions, with Portrait. Complete in 3 vols., 5*s.* each.

Vol. I. contains "Songs of Two Worlds." Vol. II. contains "The Epic of Hades." Vol. III. contains "Gwen" and "The Ode of Life."

MORRIS, Lewis—continued.

The Epic of Hades. With 16 Autotype Illustrations, after the Drawings of the late George R. Chapman. 4to, cloth extra, gilt leaves, 25*s*.

The Epic of Hades. Presentation Edition. 4to, cloth extra, gilt leaves, 10*s*. 6*d*.

Ode of Life, The. Fourth Edition. Crown 8vo, 5*s*.

Songs Unsung. Fcap. 8vo.

MORSHEAD, E. D. A.—**The House of Atreus.** Being the Agamemnon, Libation-Bearers, and Furies of Æschylus. Translated into English Verse. Crown 8vo, 7*s*.

The Suppliant Maidens of Æschylus. Crown 8vo, 3*s*. 6*d*.

NADEN, Constance W.—**Songs and Sonnets of Spring Time.** Small crown 8vo, 5*s*.

NEWELL, E. J.—**The Sorrows of Simona and Lyrical Verses.** Small crown 8vo, 3*s*. 6*d*.

NOAKE, Major R. Compton.—**The Bivouac**; or, Martial Lyrist. With an Appendix: Advice to the Soldier. Fcap. 8vo, 5*s*. 6*d*.

NOEL, The Hon. Roden.—**A Little Child's Monument.** Second Edition. Small crown 8vo, 3*s*. 6*d*.

NORRIS, Rev. Alfred.—**The Inner and Outer Life. Poems.** Fcap. 8vo, 6*s*.

O'HAGAN, John.—**The Song of Roland.** Translated into English Verse. New and Cheaper Edition. Crown 8vo, 5*s*.

PFEIFFER, Emily.—**Glan Alarch**: His Silence and Song: a Poem. Second Edition. Crown 8vo, 6*s*.

Gerard's Monument, and other Poems. Second Edition. Crown 8vo, 6*s*.

Quarterman's Grace, and other Poems. Crown 8vo, 5*s*.

Poems. Second Edition. Crown 8vo, 6*s*.

Sonnets and Songs. New Edition. 16mo, handsomely printed and bound in cloth, gilt edges, 4*s*.

Under the Aspens; Lyrical and Dramatic. With Portrait. Crown 8vo, 6*s*.

PIKE, Warburton.—**The Inferno of Dante Allighieri.** Demy 8vo, 5*s*.

POE, Edgar Allan.—**Poems.** With an Essay on his Poetry by ANDREW LANG, and a Frontispiece by Linley Sambourne. Parchment Library Edition, 6*s*.; vellum, 7*s*. 6*d*.

Rare Poems of the 16th and 17th Centuries. Edited W. J. LINTON. Crown 8vo, 5*s*.

RHOADES, James.—**The Georgics of Virgil.** Translated into English Verse. Small crown 8vo, 5*s*.

ROBINSON, A. Mary F.—**A Handful of Honeysuckle.** Fcap. 8vo, 3*s*. 6*d*.

The Crowned Hippolytus. Translated from Euripides. With New Poems. Small crown 8vo, 5*s*.

SAUNDERS, John.—**Love's Martyrdom.** A Play and Poem. Small crown 8vo, 5*s*.

Schiller's Mary Stuart. German Text, with English Translation on opposite page by LEEDHAM WHITE. Crown 8vo, 6*s*.

SCOTT, George F. E.—**Theodora and other Poems.** Small 8vo, 3*s*. 6*d*.

SELKIRK, J. B.—**Poems.** Crown 8vo, 7*s*. 6*d*.

Shakspere's Sonnets. Edited by EDWARD DOWDEN. With a Frontispiece etched by Leopold Lowenstam, after the Death Mask. Parchment Library Edition, 6*s*.; vellum, 7*s*. 6*d*.

Shakspere's Works. Complete in 12 Volumes. Parchment Library Edition, 6*s*. each; vellum, 7*s*. 6*d*. each.

SHAW, W. F., M.A.—**Juvenal, Persius, Martial, and Catullus.** An Experiment in Translation. Crown 8vo, 5*s*.

SHELLEY, Percy Bysshe.—**Poems Selected from.** Dedicated to Lady Shelley. With Preface by RICHARD GARNETT. Parchment Library Edition, 6*s*.; vellum, 7*s*. 6*d*.

Six Ballads about King Arthur. Crown 8vo, extra, gilt edges, 3*s*. 6*d*.

SLADEN, Douglas B.—**Frithjof and Ingebjorg, and other Poems.** Small crown 8vo, 5*s*.

TAYLOR, Sir H.—**Works.** Complete in Five Volumes. Crown 8vo, 30*s*.

Philip Van Artevelde. Fcap. 8vo, 3*s*. 6*d*.

The Virgin Widow, etc. Fcap. 8vo, 3*s*. 6*d*.

The Statesman. Fcap. 8vo, 3*s*. 6*d*.

TENNYSON, Alfred.—Works Complete:—

The Imperial Library Edition. Complete in 7 vols. Demy 8vo, 10*s*. 6*d*. each; in Roxburgh binding, 12*s*. 6*d*. each.

Author's Edition. In 7 vols. Post 8vo, gilt 43*s*. 6*d*.; or half-morocco, Roxburgh style, 54*s*.

Cabinet Edition. 13 vols. Each with Frontispiece. Fcap. 8vo, 2*s*. 6*d*. each.

Cabinet Edition. 13 vols. Complete in handsome Ornamental Case. 35*s*.